D0099310

Work in Progress

Work in Progress

UNCONVENTIONAL THOUGHTS ON DESIGNING AN EXTRAORDINARY LIFE

LEANNE FORD
AND STEVE FORD

W PUBLISHING GROUP

AN IMPRINT OF THOMAS NELSON

Published in Nashville, Tennessee, by W Publishing, an imprint of Thomas Nelson.

Thomas Nelson titles may be purchased in bulk for educational, business, fund-raising, or sales promotional use. For information, please e-mail SpecialMarkets@ThomasNelson.com.

Any Internet addresses, phone numbers, or company or product information printed in this book are offered as a resource and are not intended in any way to be or to imply an endorsement by Thomas Nelson, nor does Thomas Nelson vouch for the existence, content, or services of these sites, phone numbers, companies, or products beyond the life of this book.

ISBN 978-0-7852-2614-7 (HC)
ISBN 978-0-78652-2623-9 (eBook)

Library of Congress Cataloging-in-Publication Data

Library of Congress Control Number: 2019947011

Printed in the United States of America
19 20 21 22 23 LSC 10 9 8 7 6 5 4 3 2 1

There is no such thing as a "self-made (wo)man." We get to where we're going through the support of our communities—of the ones who helped us, let alone the ones who raised us. And the One who created us.

We can never take credit for where we are today. We can only thank all the people who nudged us forward step-by-step. There's very rarely a massive leap; it's mainly a series of baby steps, and one day you look back and think, Wow! How did I get this far? *And you can see a thousand beautiful and friendly faces smiling and waving at you, and a few not-so-friendly faces that helped you move forward just as much, if not more, than the kind ones.*

So to all of you, we say thank you.

It is not the critic who counts; not the man who points out how the strong man stumbles, or where the doer of deeds could've done them better. The credit belongs to the man who is actually in the arena, whose face is marred by dust and sweat and blood; who strives valiantly; who errs, who comes short again and again, because there is no effort without error and shortcoming; but who does actually strive to do the deeds; who knows great enthusiasms, the great devotions; who spends himself in a worthy cause; who at the best knows in the end the triumph of great achievement, and who at the worst, if he fails, at least fails while daring greatly, so that his place shall never be with those cold and timid souls who neither know victory nor defeat.

–TEDDY ROOSEVELT

Contents

FOREWORD

No Guts, No Glory!

This was one of our dad's favorite sayings for us growing up. Our dad had several sayings that I'm sure Leanne and Steve will share in the coming chapters. (Spoiler alert: my favorite was "Don't major in minors.") But in many ways, "No guts, no glory" has been an ongoing theme in the lives of the Ford family.

Let me tell you, Steve and Leanne have some major guts. As the oldest of three kids, I had a front-row seat to many of Steve and Leanne's "adventures," and naturally, our childhood had a profound impact on the people we are today.

I tend to field a lot of questions about our childhood. As the older sister, I am the one people ask about what Steve and Leanne were like when we were growing up. Did we always get along? Were they always creative? How did they get a show? Steve is so tall! How tall is he? Why does Leanne love white paint so much?

I can tell you that growing up in the suburbs of Pittsburgh in the '80s and '90s, we had the blessing of being raised in a loving home where creativity was encouraged, rules were set, and faith was the foundation. In many ways, our parents made us feel that the Ford family was a team. While friends are important, family is everything.

I'm three years older than Steve, and one of my favorite memories of him was playing on our driveway on a blistering hot summer's day. Steve was around the age of four, and he taught himself to ride a bike without training wheels. A bunch of older neighborhood kids were watching in awe as Steve defied the odds by riding a two-wheel bike at such a young age. Steve was, and still is, in constant motion.

As a kid, Steve was always building and taking apart his toys, playing in the woods, building go-karts, riding his BMX bike, building ramps, climbing trees, and doing what boys did in those days. Steve and I loved pro wrestling's Hulk Hogan; the movies *E.T.*, *Star Wars*, and *Bill & Ted's Excellent Adventure*; and watching *The Dukes of Hazzard* on Friday nights and *Pee-wee's Playhouse* on Saturday mornings. We'd play *Mario Bros.* and *Contra* for hours on his Nintendo.

I remember being little kids in our church's kids choir during an annual Christmas performance. I was around ten years old; I was dressed as an angel and was singing my heart out. Steve, age seven, would lie across the risers out of boredom, refusing to sing in the choir. The choir director would get so mad at him, but every Christmas concert it was the same deal. The director finally got smart and made Steve one of the wise men, so he'd make his appearance and then disappear into the wings.

One of my favorite memories about Leanne was when she was born. I was six, and I was beyond thrilled that "we" were expecting a baby. It was like a little-kid dream come true. I distinctly recall insisting that we name the baby Bongo. I have no idea where that came from, but it seemed like a good idea to my six-year-old mind. I remember my parents calling us from the hospital when she was born; we were at our Grandma and Grandpa Williams's house. When I found out they had named the baby Leanne and not Bongo, I was a bit brokenhearted. But that disappointment quickly melted away and was replaced by pure joy of having a new baby sister.

Steve and I were literally jumping for joy on my grandparents' screened-in patio that night. We celebrated with fudge sundaes, and it was a night I'll never forget.

My parents came home from the hospital with Leanne on July 4. I was so happy and felt like the fireworks we saw that night were in celebration of Leanne's arrival.

Leanne was the shyest kid I ever knew. We're talking painfully shy. For the first four to five years of her life, she really only talked to my mom. We would have babysitters, and Leanne would cry in the corner to protest my mom leaving. I could try to console or distract her, but it was no use. She was as stubborn as she was shy.

I also remember the time that, at age five or so, she was playing in the basement with a neighborhood friend named Greg, and they came upstairs for a snack and to show off their new "haircuts." Leanne had given herself and Greg new "bangs," and wow, it was awful. Leanne's bangs were so short in patches, and Greg's hack-styled hair had a similar vibe.

I'm not sure if Greg's mom ever recovered, but my mom didn't lose her cool, and I was impressed. Leanne went on to get a mullet haircut, and all in all, I remember being shocked that Leanne would do such a thing—with safety scissors, no less! While she was quiet, Leanne was always a little rebel in her own way.

While I have so many fun memories of us growing up, our favorite shared experience was our yearly summer tradition of going to a family camp called Deer Valley YMCA Family Camp for one week each summer. The camp is nestled in the hills of Pennsylvania, and for our family it was a slice of heaven.

Steve would do a countdown before we'd go to Deer Valley each year. The night before leaving, Steve wouldn't be able to sleep; he'd be so excited. And it's no wonder. Deer Valley was awesome. On any given day you could go sailing, fishing, rock climbing, hiking, and horseback riding. The camp had a community feel, with camp counselors and the families who would come year after year. It was a safe place where we could be ourselves.

At Deer Valley, we got messy. We could hike and swim and do tie-dye or throw a clay pot, all in the same day. These types of adventures would require us to get outside and be creative, and they would be messy. Our parents didn't mind in the slightest. They knew that getting dirty was just good, clean fun. At Deer Valley, we would be silly. We didn't care the least about being cool. Family camp included singing camp songs, eating together in a dining hall, and all sorts of group activities—and we loved it! Most important, at Deer Valley, we could be together as a family. There was no television, and there were no video games or distractions from the outside world.

Steve, Leanne, and I ended up working as counselors in our teens and early twenties, and we still enjoy going to this day. Deer Valley is a magical place, and it is a big part of who we are and what we love.

Cut ahead to the past five years, and life certainly got more interesting when Steve and Leanne started to collaborate on restoration projects in our hometown of Pittsburgh, Pennsylvania. Leanne had a lived-in style that was fresh and inspiring and breathed new life into the most dismal of spaces. Steve had the ability, skill, and grit to turn Leanne's grand vision into a reality (no small feat). I knew they were onto something special.

I wasn't totally surprised when Leanne told me that she was having discussions with a production company about a possible HGTV collaboration. Leanne was always meeting interesting people and doing interesting things in her career and as a part of her artistic pursuits. She had a knack for connecting with people, and people seemed to be drawn to her.

What surprised me was that Steve was part of the pitch. Don't get me wrong; Steve is awesome, and he is beyond talented—but he is a man of few words. I called Steve and said something along the lines of, "You know you need to talk, *a lot*, if you're interested in doing this, right?" But he was game and intrigued about the opportunity. Steve was always fearless as a river guide or skiing on the slopes, but this business of doing a brother/sister show for a major network was certainly blazing a new trail.

When I look back, it seemed as if it took years for *Restored by the Fords* to become a reality. Steve and Leanne had interviews and conference calls and did "sizzle reels," whatever that is, to see how they would come across on camera. I didn't tell anyone what was going on until the *Restored by the Fords* pilot episode aired in December 2016. I knew the odds of a show coming to fruition would be one in a million, but I believed in Leanne's innovative vision and Steve's creative contracting.

The first episode of season 1 aired on a bitterly cold Tuesday night in January 2018. Family, friends, workers, and clients from the season gathered in a former gymnasium at the Ace Hotel in Pittsburgh. The show was projected on the wall, and we watched with nervous anticipation—laughing together at Leanne and Steve's on-air antics, joking with each other during the commercial breaks, and applauding during the big reveal at the end.

Happiness swept over me that night. The home they restored on the show looked amazing, and the client seemed thrilled. I expected that. But what really got me was the show captured Steve and Leanne—not just their work, but their personalities, their demeanor, and their authentic selves. Pittsburghers are as real as they come, and to me, *that* was the mark of success.

Steve and Leanne's journey hasn't been easy, expected, or typical. But they are the hardest-working people I know. They have inspired me in so many ways. While their story is still unfolding, they have the guts, talent, and bravery to follow their own paths. The glory, for them, is the ability to do what they love, and love what they do.

Michelle Ford Faist
Written at Deer Valley YMCA Family Camp
July 3, 2018

PROLOGUE

Never Too Late

Leanne

Julia Child didn't realize her passion for French cooking until she was thirty-six.[1] Van Gogh didn't even know he could paint until he was twenty-seven.[2] Robert Frost didn't hit his stride as a poet until his forties.[3] And not to put myself even close to being in the same category as those artists, but for the record, I didn't do my first official interior design project until I was past thirty. And I would use that word *official* very loosely. Steve? Well, Steve is out on a river or mountain somewhere and couldn't be reached for questioning.

The list goes on and on of people we look up to, compare our lives to, our art to, who just didn't have it together quite the way we think they did. We think we should know what we are doing by now. We think we should know what we *want* to be doing by now. We think we should have found what we are good at by now. But why? Life is an evolution, and while we are still on the planet, it's never too late to pursue your next dream. So give yourself a break! Relax and enjoy the creative process otherwise known as life.

———

People ask us all the time how Steve and I got here. From my perspective, "here" is just part of our story; it's not the end of it, and it's certainly not the beginning. How did two kids from a traditional home in Pittsburgh start a successful business fixing up old houses in their hometown, and then land a national TV show?

The truth is, we got here because of the love and support of others. We got here because of all the people along that way who saw something in us, believed in us, encouraged us, and pushed us forward. Since childhood, we have always been encouraged to take risks.

Well, actually, that's less true for Steve, as his risks were climbing buildings and towers and such, so maybe Steve was encouraged to take fewer risks. But still!

We both live with a sort of freedom inside us. We were never afraid to fail. In fact, we got here by failing and failing a lot. We found things we weren't good at; we tried things that didn't work; I may or may not have been fired more than once. (Okay, twice.) We've been knocked down, but we always seem to pop back up, dust ourselves off, and keep cruising. We kept looking for what gives us inner joy, for our reason to get up in the morning, searching for what we were naturally good at. We got here by being ourselves and forging our own paths. (For me, that path comment is a figurative statement; for Steve, it's quite literal.)

Steve and I grew up in the suburbs of Pittsburgh. Our mom stayed at home; Dad was a lawyer. Three kids. Dinner every night at 6:00 p.m., and church on Sunday. I guess you could say we were the quintessential suburban family. And here we are, finishing up our twenty-fifth home design and construction for our show, *Restored by the Fords*, in our hometown. Recently, life has been a whirlwind, to say the least.

My favorite part of it all, though? I'd like to think Steve and I are helping people figure out how to design and love their homes, and to me that's a true pleasure. And if we get some smiles and laughs along the way, then that's all the better.

It's July 2018, and I'm moving out of my schoolhouse. The schoolhouse, built in 1906 and set back in the woods, surrounded by one-hundred-foot oaks, is where I've been living for eight years. This is the first house I ever designed. Back at the turn of the twentieth century, this building was the only school for the small town of Sewickley, Pennsylvania. It's still got the bell to prove it.

My design team and I move back and forth out of the house; we are wrapping trinkets and packing up my collections. You can collect a lot in eight years. The schoolhouse is full-on Americana: American flags. Deer antlers. An old black-and-white photo of Johnny Cash standing next to a sharply dressed Billy Graham hangs next to me as I write. This place is about history. It's full of trinkets, baskets, bottles, and other special treasures I've found along the way. My friends call me the "house whisperer" because I always try to listen to the house when exploring how best to evolve its style. This house is no exception. It's 100 percent Americana. It told me so.

My schoolhouse is the place where I first discovered my interior design chops; it's where I could finally try out new ideas. In this old, dusty place, I began to get serious about taking design risks. I turned an attic crawl space into a grand master bathroom, despite three contractors telling me it was impossible. That very bathroom became famous. It was photographed for the cover of a design book, appeared in magazine after magazine, and was pinned on Pinterest thousands of times.

This house has had quite the life. The bands Escondido and the Lone Bellow have written songs here that ended up on their albums. Lord Huron, Rayland Baxter, Nikki Lane, Shirock, Among Savages, Rosi Golan, Odessa, and many other singers and bands have drunk wine, written music, and slept here en route to Nashville or New York.

Yep, this house has lived a great life. And this house started it all for me.

But it's time to pass this gem on to a new family. I'm moving into a 1950s midcentury-modern ranch that's currently in a state of, well, chaos. I love the new place. It's on seven acres and set back into the woods. I've got no neighbors. Give me those country roads any day of the week.

I've also decided to go with something entirely different when decorating this house: minimalism. I'm a girl who likes my stuff, but I am also drawn to clean lines and simplicity. So this will be an interesting challenge for me. I'll let the house guide my process, like I always do.

In addition to moving and designing my new home and renovating homes for the show, I'm also three months pregnant.

You could say I'm taking on a lot.

My husband, Erik Allen Ford (who, by the way, recently changed his last name to mine—so sweet, right?), was concerned about our moving into a new house. "You're taking on another project on top of a season of projects?" he said. This coming from a man who understands creative projects: Erik is the cofounder of the menswear brand Buck Mason.

Right now, Erik and I are living a rather disjointed life. I'm working on the show five days a week, which includes filming, decorating houses, and, yes, being a chipper on-air television personality.

Erik flies in every weekend. Arrives Thursday, leaves Monday. I try to go to Los Angeles when I can, but it's a little bit harder. My husband's company is based on the West Coast, and it's not like we can uproot the whole company. (Believe me: I asked!) As much as I consider myself a nomad, we don't like missing each other. But we've learned to appreciate the particular riches of the two lives we live—one in Pittsburgh and one in Los Angeles.

Recently, Erik changed his mind about me taking on too much. "Decorating our new house is your respite from it all," he said. He understood.

And he's right. Decorating is what feels good to me. It's what re-energizes me. It feels right to work on my own place. I'm putting so much energy into everyone else's homes. In my house, I get to take risks, try new ideas.

It's important to open your mind to something new and to have a new way of thinking. I can't wait to live in this minimalist house, to walk around my simple, uncluttered home. The place I can escape from it all. My new beginning.

Steve's place, though? Now, that's another story.

Steve

The front door of my building reads: "Don't come here."

Leanne

If you can call it a front door, considering it's in a back alley.

Steve

I moved into this building, which is in a hilly neighborhood just south of downtown Pittsburgh, in April 2018. This area of Pittsburgh has its own history. Throughout the late 1800s and early 1900s, it was filled with folks, mostly immigrants, who worked in the iron and steel mills. Once the mills shut down, more people moved out of the area. Recently, though, artists and musicians have breathed some life into the neighborhood: we've got a heavy metal coffee shop just down the road, a punk rock record store, and, yes, even a vegan café. I guess what I'm saying is that it's become kind of a cool and affordable place to live, especially if you're an artist who doesn't have a lot of money. And especially if you like a gritty, industrial vibe. Which I do.

And that's what attracted me most to my new place, a former heavy-machinery factory. You can still see the factory's original name in cracked old red letters painted over the exterior's yellowish brick. We've got a service entrance and a rickety wooden ramp that takes you up to the main floor, where me and my friends—Ed Zeiler, Bobby Benson, and Doug Pritts, who are regulars on the show—work on projects or sometimes even throw knives at a large wooden target board. (No—we never use people for targets!) Downstairs is where Ed and I keep our collection of old mopeds and motorcycles; we have about eight of them lined up in a row. (We used to call ourselves a moped gang—more on that later.) There's a large storage room where Leanne keeps her stuff from all her projects. Shortly after I gave her the space, I had to literally build walls to hold all her stuff. Otherwise she'd completely take over! (Sorry, Leanne.) We're working on bulding a spray room with ventilation too. Right now, cabinet doors hang in the service entrance downstairs like mobiles in the wind, as we let the paint dry.

I wanted a place with a soul that could be a source of creativity for me and my buddies. At first, some people told me it was crazy to buy this building. They thought I'd gone off the deep end. But it turns out this space is exactly what I needed. As soon as you start doing a project or working together with your friends, you get inspired. My friends are always here at my shop, either working on a project or hanging out. A lot of times I'll say, "Ed, you have to go home, man. You worked hard. Now go to your family." (He spends a lot of time with his family—promise!) But it's easy to stay here. It's a lot like a clubhouse.

I tell all my guys who don't have a shop: "If you want to do something, come over and do it here." I don't want to be in here just making stuff by myself. I want to be surrounded by people making things as well. For me it's about bringing groups of people together. I'd rather share it than do it on my own.

We're in the middle of construction. Leanne is going to decorate the living space for me, because of course she is. I'm giving her no choice in the matter. You can say Leanne and I live parallel lives. We are both starting something new—just in the most opposite ways imaginable.

Her new place is a minimalist 1950s-style house in the country. My new place is a former heavy-machinery factory in the middle of the city.

Now I'm renovating this 7,000-square-foot space into my shop and my living space. My living space, above my shop, is 1,800 square feet. Down the street is a small, run-down shack. It's a little white house. Not much to it. It might sound crazy, but my dream is to buy that place and turn it into a drive-thru coffee shop. That might not happen, but we'll see.

My mom wasn't thrilled when I showed her my new place. The door is what my mom first noticed. Talk about an interesting first impression!

"I'd prefer it if you lived in the suburbs," she said. A true mother's dream.

But I think Mom ultimately gets why I'm here. She knows this place fits my personality. People's dogs or cars and houses represent who they are. This factory represents me pretty well, and the dirt and graffiti don't bother me at all. I also happen to be the proud parent of the best pit bull around! I know that my mom wasn't thrilled about that choice either, but Yoko, my rescued pit bull, really is perfect for me.

Before I bought the place, there were four feet of weeds growing up the hill next to the factory. It was overgrown and looked abandoned. Now there's a place for Yoko to go out. Yoko's a funny dog. She's kind of my little junkyard dog who is a total sweetheart but likes to bark at anyone who passes by the fence. She's the defender of my castle.

You can't find a building like mine anywhere in Pittsburgh, let alone the suburbs, for what I paid for it. For me, it's the perfect space. Especially since Leanne is decorating it; I know what Leanne is capable of, and I have high expectations.

I ended up spending a whole chunk of money on renovating my space, and it was worth every penny. I was involved in designing practically everything, from the layout to the black tile in my steam shower. I'm really proud of how it came out.

Right now, the metal factory windows are all blown out. I call it the "open-air concept." You have to understand that I *like* being rugged. Not having windows doesn't bother me. Yes, it was a little bit cold, so I bought a wood-burning stove. Started a fire. (I was fine.) It's like camping—actually, it's more like *Survivor*. Yep, this is my version of *Survivor*, and roughing it will make the final transformation of my living space that much sweeter.

I'd rented so many places before this. I rented a garage. I rented an apartment. I rented a store. I really just didn't want to rent anymore. I wanted to settle down. I wanted to find one place where I could have it all. So now I have this place, my diamond in the rough.

The show has given me some new opportunities, but nothing has changed too much yet. I still do my laundry at the Laundromat. I'm a couple of weeks away from having a washer and dryer. Doing my laundry—all Buck Mason T-shirts, of course—at the Laundromat doesn't bother me, because I've been doing my laundry at the Laundromat for twenty years. I actually do own a washer and dryer, but until my sister designs my place, they're not going in.

I walked into this place, and everything was wet with mildew. All the windows were covered or broken. It looked like a hoarder lived here. But I looked at it and saw the potential. I thought, *Wow! This is awesome.* I've never bought a building in my life. I've been waiting for this place. If you walked inside it now, in its unfinished state—the before state, if you will; the state before my sister gets to it—you might think I was crazy buying it. It's completely raw. There aren't even walls. But I looked at houses, and I said to myself, *This isn't me.* I don't want to live in a house. I don't want to live in the suburbs. I don't want to live next to another house. This place came up, and I *knew* this was it.

Leanne

Steve and I are very different. We can drive each other crazy, but as much as I hate to admit this, it's probably that very yin and yang that creates great projects and, therefore, a great show. We may take different approaches, but we have one thing in common: we're both 100 percent, certifiably, undeniably unafraid of failure. In fact, it seems we've failed our way right into success.

We're both on completely new adventures. We both have new homes. We're filming season 2 of the show. As I write, Steve and I are eight days away from revealing his factory remodel to Mom and Michelle. And Erik and I are about to become parents.

Sharing how we remodel homes with the HGTV audience has been incredibly exciting for us. But how we ended up here feels like a bit of a whirlwind. I speak to people all the time, and they're always asking us how we decided to film the show in Pittsburgh.

Well, why not Pittsburgh? It's where we were born and raised!

Steve

My heart has always been here in Pittsburgh. The longest I was gone was a year straight. There were two years where I drove back and forth from LA to Pittsburgh about eight times. Crazy, I know.

Leanne

I was living in Los Angeles, falling in love with my now husband, Erik, and working on my design business. I never thought that this show would bring me back to Pittsburgh.

Or maybe I did.

Steve

This city is steeped in history, which is pretty cool. And the Ford family sort of belongs here. I think Dad would be happy we're here, using our talent and creativity to make this place better. Also, another interesting fact: Dad grew up right around the corner from my building. I guess you could say he's always with me.

Leanne

Dad died in 2004. And Steve's right: Dad would have been thrilled that we're here, filming our show in Pittsburgh, renovating houses together and giving people a new future and a place they love to live in.

But for Steve and me, this book is about more than just how we're transforming houses in Pittsburgh. It's so much more than that! This book is about how two kids from a traditional home in Pittsburgh were able to go out in this world and follow our crazy dreams. I mentioned earlier that people ask us all the time how we got here. Besides the love and support we've received along the way, we got here by taking a lot of risks, by not being afraid to fail.

A huge reason why we had the confidence to follow these very strange but fun paths that we're on is because of our parents. Mom and Dad gave us the grounding we needed and then the freedom we needed to become who we are.

We feel so lucky and thrilled to share all of this with you. We hope that you'll find this book helpful in creating a life—and a home—that lasts, something that you can love forever, that you can be proud of, and, most importantly, that you can enjoy.

1

Avocado Be Gone!

> I am going to make everything around
> me beautiful. That will be my life.
>
> —ELSIE DE WOLFE

Leanne

We grew up in a suburb just thirty minutes outside of Pittsburgh, with rolling hills and crabapple trees and modern brick houses built to last. We had a lucky life growing up; we were always insulated and cared for. Our mom still lives in the same house we grew up in. I've spent so many of my adult years moving around the country, throwing everything I own into the car and redecorating each old rental along the way. I felt comfortable doing that, I think, because Mom's house was my safety net. I always knew I had our childhood home to go back to.

Mom's style was traditional, with a hint of trend. But when she decorated her house, she took creative risks.

Growing up, we had an Asian-themed living room. Peach-white walls and rice wallpaper. You could see the lines in the matching peach plush carpet from where Mom vacuumed. This room was considered off-limits, except for special occasions. Then there was the bamboo furniture and Asian four-panel silk screens. We had two matching couches facing each other, covered with images of bamboo trees and Japanese blooms.

The peach-hued Asian-themed living room, which, our mom wants you to know, has since been updated, remained for thirty years. "Mom, you've had this living room so long that you've gone out of *and* come back into style," I told her once. "If you keep waiting, you'll be back." Mom was ahead of her time *four times* in thirty years.

It's also worth noting that the artificial Christmas tree in the living room always matched the color story and theme of the room. The ornaments were peach. The ribbons were peach. Everything on that tree was peach. It was Mom's pride and joy—besides us, I hope. (But who can be sure?)

Now, the tree in the family room was a different story. This is where the *real* Christmas tree lived. And it was a free-for-all. This was the big one, covered with all the colored lights three kids could dream of. We threw every single ornament we'd ever made or collected up on that gem of a tree.

My bedroom also had a theme: let's call it "French country." I'm talking Laura Ashley bedding and pink-and-white striped wallpaper with a floral border—all of which I passionately chose in the eighth grade. The furniture was (and is) matching white wicker. I decided on a rocking chair with white pillows, pink tassels, and lace, along with a narrow, white wicker highboy dresser. If you open the lowest drawer and stick your head underneath it, you will see the list of all the cute boys' names I had written down on the bottom side. I'd get down on the floor, slide my body beneath the open drawers, and scribble names on the wood in red pen: "I ❤ William 1/23/96." My teenage heart, engraved on the bottom of a drawer.

A little note card on my door reads: "The Laura Ashley Room." This was a recent touch my mom made five or six years ago. She calls it her little bed-and-breakfast. When her friends and sisters come to stay, they get to experience the first room I designed. (I'd like to apologize to my relatives for going with a twin bed.)

The kitchen at my parents' house was also very traditional, with a few trends thrown in. With its dark brown wooden cabinets, jungle wallpaper, and natural cane cantilever chairs—you know the ones—it was somethin' else. All of the appliances were avocado green, which was a hot color in the 1970s! We make fun of those appliances now, but when Mom picked them out, she was cutting-edge.

I think about those avocado appliances when I'm designing people's homes. The truth is, we really should avoid trendy appliances. Your appliances have to last for years. They're one of the major expenses in your kitchen, so they should be classic and simple. Let your wild, artistic side come out in other ways. Although sometimes I break that rule—as I do all rules, even my own.

There I was, twelve years old, with only one design project—my Laura Ashley room—under my belt. But I knew something in that kitchen was wrong. Very wrong. As in, the refrigerator. Our avocado-hued refrigerator was quite simply the wrong color. It was the first time that my sense of right and wrong coincided with my natural instinct for design.

No one expected me to become an interior designer. Mom thought I was going to be the principal of a school, or a judge. But I started noticing design in other families' homes. I realized that there were better refrigerator colors out there.

One day I had an epiphany: our refrigerator needed to be white.

Kids are often more intuitive than we give them credit for. Mom understood this. She was big on listening to our ideas. She didn't shut me down if I had a crazy suggestion.

We had a lot of freedom to create projects. For instance, I used to collect old, used candles and leftover candle wax to make new candles. I would spend an afternoon melting down candles in Mom's pots. My mom's reaction: "That's a fun project, honey!" When I was done melting down candles in the pots, Mom would just throw the pots away. Then she would go to Goodwill, buy some more old pots, and let me melt more candles in them. Recently, one of my sister Michelle's friends asked her, "Is Leanne still making candles in the house?" (My answer is yes, by the way.) That was her strongest memory of me. Michelle called me "pioneer lady."

We had a balance of real boundaries with our parents, but they also gave us so much freedom. There were rules, restrictions, yes. But not when it came to our imagination. Mister Rogers was from Pittsburgh, so that concept of "I like you just the way you are"[1] rubbed off on our family. It really was my parents' philosophy.

When I was in the fifth grade, I had a school project where we were told to make a business card, a slogan, and a logo. I was working with Dad, designing the business card, and Dad asked me what my slogan was.

"My name is Leanne. If I want to, I can."

Dad laughed proudly; he was so impressed that he ran to tell Mom. That slogan became, in a way, a slogan of my life. My family still quotes it to me when they want to tease me.

Anyway, one day, I came home from school and stared at that ugly avocado-colored fridge. I turned to Mom and said, "Let's paint the refrigerator white."

Mom's response: "You can't actually paint refrigerators."

"Yes, you can," I said. "I'm sure you can."

(My name is Leanne. If I want to, I can.)

Maybe, just maybe, it's possible that I took my little "my name is Leanne" pep talk one step too far. I felt invincible—if I just put my mind to it, I could create it. Funny, I still have that same outlook about decorating. It's what Steve and I argue about most.

Steve

Exactly. Just the other day, for instance, Leanne gave me a ten-foot door to put on an eight-foot wall.

Leanne

"Cut it down two feet," I told him. "Let's make it work!"

Steve

It doesn't really work that way, Leanne. First off, you have to frame the opening. Then I may have to reframe the whole wall. Then the door is eight inches wide instead of five inches wide. And then we have to build a whole new wall out on the inside.

She sees it like this: "Oh, the door is pretty. That's the door we need."

Leanne

So you're saying it *does* work, Steve . . .

I will say this: as the youngest of three, I had to fight for what I thought was right. I'm still that way. If it's the door we need, then it's only right that we *get that door.*

I've been like this with everyone in my family as long as I can remember. When I was around fifteen, for example, Mom had become a little, let's say, lackadaisical about wrapping Christmas presents. It was a slow degradation. At first she would write the name of the gift on the back side of the label. (Like, *Sweater* or *Monopoly*—which, by the way, was banned from our house because we had the biggest fights ever over that game.) To me, this was injustice. Writing the presents on the label killed the surprise—it ruined the joy of Christmas! That was just the beginning. A couple of years later, she didn't even *hide* the wrapped presents. I would have to wrap a few of them myself. I was only fifteen. I had at least three more years of real kid time left!

I would go through those presents and write my name on the gifts. *Oh, there's a new bike. Label that* Leanne.

Wait a second. I was handy, but this was ridiculous!

"Still a kid over here!" I finally said. "Mom, please hide the Christmas presents!"

Again, it didn't matter if it was the injustice of unwrapped Christmas gifts or if I was fighting with Steve over the size of a door. I wasn't good at backing down. (I'm still not.) If I saw an unfairness, I'd fight to change it. (Hence, why my parents thought I should be a judge or a lawyer.)

But anyway . . . where were we? Refrigerator. When I was ten and I saw that avocado-colored refrigerator, I knew I could paint it. I knew we *must* paint it. *No one* was going to tell me any different.

Except, maybe, Dad.

Dad could put the kibosh on painting the refrigerator. Mom had gotten on board with painting it white. She loved the idea. She agreed that we could figure out some solution to paint it, but she needed to clear it with Dad first. So Mom and I went to Dad to deliver the news.

"Dad, I have a great idea. I want to paint the refrigerator white," I said, my face glowing, my dimples perking, and my mother by my side.

"Absolutely not," Dad said. "You're not going to ruin a perfectly good working appliance."

Mom wasn't thrilled about this. She wanted us to have freedom about our choices. I got that from her. I'm not afraid to try something new. And—let's admit it—she wanted a white fridge! Steve is probably more like my dad in that he questions the practicality of things. I always think, *Well, why not try it?* Which was precisely Mom's thinking: *Who was it hurting to paint the refrigerator white?*

I look at renovating houses the same way. I tell people to look at the bigger picture. I ask this of people all the time when they're making a big change: What is the greater good of the project?

"We're all stuck in concrete," Mom said when we recently discussed the refrigerator story. "We don't like change. We like the status quo. Creating is all about getting out of the box, and we don't like to get out of the box."

Dad had no idea how to paint a refrigerator; therefore, he decided it couldn't be done. He refused to even consider it.

Steve

Generally, though, both our parents were open-minded. They gave us any opportunity that we wanted. They were supportive of us. It wasn't like they said, "Here's a paintbrush." But they did say, "Oh, if you want a paintbrush, we'll help you and run out and get one."

Leanne

Except in the case of the refrigerator. Dad certainly wasn't buying any paintbrushes for that project.

But then Dad left town for the weekend. *(Insert sneaky laugh here.)* He and Steve, who was about thirteen at the time, went on a ski trip together.

Knowing me, I probably pushed the issue. I probably walked by that avocado-colored refrigerator, felt disgusted by its presence, and convinced myself that it had to go and it *had to go now.* I was a persistent kid. It's a great quality to have as an adult. As a kid—not as much. Persistent kids can get themselves into trouble. But this time I had an ally: Mom.

Of course, Mom had to be on my side. I was only ten. After all, someone had to buy the paint!

I had seen an article in a home improvement magazine about how to paint your refrigerator. It was fate. We went to the hardware store, got what we needed, and while Steve and Dad were skiing in Colorado, we painted that ugly thing. We worked through the middle of the night, like little elves; it had to dry before they got home.

It was G-rated sneaky, our secret. It was late on a Saturday night. The two of us: renegades on a mad mission.

You understand that this wasn't a professional job by any means. "We did a shabby job," Mom even admitted recently. That wasn't the point. The point is that Mom allowed me to have this vision. And if she were nervous about taking creative risks, I'm sure it would have been passed on to us. But this was a woman who put jungle wallpaper in her kitchen.

The refrigerator was built into the cabinets. Remember: I was just a little kid. Mom and I couldn't pull that refrigerator outside of the cabinet to paint the side. So we settled—we painted the door and only half of each side. When Mom got rid of the refrigerator years later, she said that the sides were half-white and half-avocado.

The refrigerator dried on Sunday, and we placed all the magnets back on it, with all the papers and photos and reminders they held in place. Pretended like nothing ever happened. Except now, we had a glorious white refrigerator.

Dad and Steve came home Sunday night, and neither of them said a word. Mom didn't even say a word until a few weeks later. "Honey, you know we painted the fridge, right?" she finally said to Dad. But remarkably, Dad never made a big deal about it. It's entirely possible that he liked the white color or didn't want to admit he was wrong. It's also possible that he didn't notice!

Steve

I noticed. I seem to remember that avocado color scraping up from under the white. I remember seeing green stuff. When you opened the fridge, you could see the avocado inside. It scratched green forever. All the magnets scratched it off.

Gotta use primer first, Leanne.

Leanne

Got it, Steve. Always use primer . . . yeah, yeah.

Painting that refrigerator was a monumental childhood moment.

For one, it was the first time I realized that painting something white will instantly improve it—in my humble opinion, of course. A few months later, I was at a party at a friend's house, and they had an all-white kitchen. It was the first white kitchen I had ever seen, and I was blown away. I had never seen white kitchen cabinets before. Our cabinets were a dark wood.

"Mom, Dad," I said, when I got back from the party, fresh off my refrigerator caper. "We have to paint these cabinets white."

"Let's do it," Mom said.

That time, we didn't do the painting ourselves. Mom hired someone to paint the cabinets. (For the record, you absolutely *can* paint your own cabinets. I've been known to do it in the past. You just have to do it right. You have to sand it, use the right paint, take the right steps. But at the end of the day, it's like painting anything else. The beauty of painting your kitchen cabinets is that it feels like you've transformed the entire room. When it's done, you feel as if you have a whole new kitchen.)

Here's the thing: Dad and Mom raised us in a way where we felt uninhibited. Painting the refrigerator didn't have dire consequences. Our creativity was appreciated and applauded, not penalized and belittled. Our ideas were considered important. We weren't just children whose voices didn't matter. Our voices mattered, and our interests mattered, and that forever impacted me and how I lived the rest of my life.

Steve

Mom and Dad gave us the best foundation we could possibly have, the perfect mix of boundaries and encouragement to explore. The way they taught us to live when we were kids has been at the root of everything we've both been able to accomplish. Most of all, they taught us to care about and strive for the right things—the things that really make life worth living.

WORKING ON PROGRESS

Here are some tips for supporting the original thinkers in your life:

1. Hear them. That's right. Don't just listen; *hear* them. Don't laugh, no matter how wild their wacky idea sounds. Just listen. Let your original thinkers–whether it's your child, your friend, your spouse, a partner–explore their ideas. Look into if it's an option; find out how it can be done.
2. Try it. Is it an invention? A song? An artistic venture? If it's something that won't hurt anyone, why not try the idea? Give it a whirl.
3. If you have the ability to help and to find or create tools to help the idea come to life–do it!
4. Let it go if they let it go. This path may not be the be-all and end-all for an original thinker. In fact, most likely it's not. So be okay with the evolution of what's next. Nothing created, thought of, or inspired is in vain.

2

Grow Slow

Play is often talked about as if it were a relief from
serious learning. But for children, play is serious
learning. . . . Play is the real work of childhood.

—MISTER ROGERS

Leanne

Mister Rogers was from Pittsburgh. He was a big part of our youth
and actually reminded me of my dad. His concept was simple—"I like
you just the way you are"—and it rubbed off on our family. This was
our family philosophy.

Many years of my childhood were spent playing school. This
wasn't just any old school; this was Michael R. Ford Elementary

School. It was located where most childhood schools are located: in the basement.

My new best friend, Elisabeth Bartelsman, and I played Michael R. Ford Elementary School together for hours.

Not just hours. For years.

Michael R. Ford Elementary was named after my dad for one reason only: we used his personalized work stationery from his law practice. It was the thick kind, with his beautiful letterhead. So it made perfect sense to name the school after our stationery.

The school was for grades K–4. We had fifty make-believe students with fifty make-believe names. We had Samantha Rose and Robbie Bustoleum. Every student had a first name and a last name, and to us they all had unique personalities. "Oh, Samantha Rose is at it again! I really can't get her to stop passing notes during class!" We would write out ten full spelling tests so we could correct ten spelling tests. We had a PTA that we may or may not have collected money from our real schoolteachers for. I think we collected nine dollars. We used my grandpa's old chalkboard to teach lessons. (I still have that chalkboard. It made an appearance in *Country Living* magazine and in Steve's house on season 2 of our show. Michael R. Ford Elementary lives on!)

We wanted an overhead projector badly. But when you're in eighth grade, you can't afford an overhead projector. So we made one. We used Mom's makeup mirror, the glass from a picture frame, and a flashlight. And it worked! That was our projector; we called him "Ollie the Overhead."

We shuttered the doors of the Michael R. Ford Elementary School at the end of high school because Mom wanted her laundry room back; she finally took the school down right before I went to college.

"You're ruining my childhood, Mom!" I told her, only half joking. Somehow, she didn't seem to care. Stone heart, I tell ya!

Steve

While Leanne was playing school, I was playing in the woods. The neighborhood we grew up in was around a lot of fairly new development. Homes were always being built on open lots and near wooded areas. So, between a group of houses, just across the street from mine, was a patch of woods.

I had a friend with a house right next to the woods, so we would be back there for hours. It was a perfect spot for a kid with an adventurous, imaginative spirit like me. It wasn't too spacious, but it was just large enough for me to get a little lost in. I would go out there and get dirty and play in creeks and build dams. I'd built forts. I created a whole other world. Mom and Dad let me play out there for hours, totally unsupervised. They knew I was safe.

Unlike Leanne, who pretended to be at school even when she wasn't at school, I didn't like school; it just didn't come natural to me. (Let's just say that my English teachers from high school will be shocked when they find out that I helped write this book. But hey, here we are.) But—surprise, surprise—I loved shop class. I couldn't be bothered with algebra or biology or academics in general, but I loved making things from nothing.

Shop class was a place in school where I excelled. And I really enjoyed home economics too. For some reason, I loved to sew, and I was good at it. I basically liked to do things with my hands.

In shop, I started out like everyone else, making a clock or a stool. But then we had the opportunity to make something that we wanted. I chose a skateboard. I ordered the trucks and the wheels, laminated five or six pieces of wood together, and painted the bottom. Threw some stickers on it. There it was: my own skateboard. It actually worked! That gave me a real sense of accomplishment.

In shop class, I could express myself in a way that felt natural. It's the same today.

According to my mom, I never complained about going to school. I guess in elementary school I was the same person I am today. I had a job to do: get through each year all the way until I finished college. It's funny because now, I basically live in a shop-class situation. I have an entire shop in my warehouse, and I love making things.

I wish I could go back and tell my fourteen-year-old self, "Hey, kid, don't worry. You're going to do what you love when you grow up." My childhood prepared me for who I am now.

Leanne

By the way, Steve, when you weren't around, I definitely went down and decorated the forts. And the tree house in the backyard. I was very stealthy about it. I'd sneak in, add a tablecloth and flowers, and pretend to put up curtains. We'd cut tree branches and place them in vases. When I was done playing, I would take everything down, removing all signs of ever being there.

Steve

That's news to me! You made it a ladies' clubhouse instead of a men's clubhouse.

Leanne

I always related to Doris Day in *Calamity Jane*. The real Calamity Jane was a frontierswoman in the 1800s. She was a pioneer. In the movie, she was the only female character *not* wearing a dress. There's a scene where Calamity Jane and her friend fix up her dingy cabin, all the while singing some chipper little tune. I related to this scene, knowing that any space, no matter how unfortunate, can be made into a home with the right touch. That's my life: fixing up old places. And sometimes singing while doing it.

Steve

Look: I just liked being outside. I still do. I would be out in the woods until it was time to come in. My sisters would run down and call for me when it was dinnertime.

I'd pretend I was Indiana Jones. We would make trails. Get on our mountain bikes. Make jumps, bridges. I was always asking my parents for strong rope to make obstacle courses and to play with. I made a skateboarding ramp. Now, I don't know that I built any *good* skateboarding ramps. I don't even think I had tools, not even a hammer and a nail. But I would most certainly stack wood, logs, brick—any materials we could find—and my friends and I would try our hardest to skate on it.

I rode mountain bikes, and sometimes BMX bikes, a lot. Again, not well, but I loved it. My friends and I made dirt tracks for mountain bikes there in the woods too. There were no distractions out there. I was completely focused. I could have been miles away, yet I was just across the street. My favorite thing really was playing outside, creating and getting dirty.

Mountain biking stuck with me throughout my teenage years. When my friends were saving money for cars, I was saving money for a mountain bike. It was my gateway to other outdoor sports. Ever since I was a kid, I've just loved that thrill of racing down mountains as fast as you can. I have so many memories of my cousin Drew and me tossing our bikes in the back of my friend's jeep and heading to a park or a mountain so we could ride down trails.

I guess your childhood does impact your future, because look at me now: I'm still playing in the dirt, still making stuff (with wood), and still biking.

Leanne

But as a rule, one thing we, the Ford kids, shouldn't play is instruments. Man oh man. I can still remember when it was time for Steve to practice his saxophone. Ouch! I would run for the hills, covering my ears. *Nooooo.* And when I practiced the flute, same torture in the house. Michelle played her violin pretty well, but still, that's not one of those instruments you only want to play "pretty well." I don't know how our parents survived three kids with zero musical ability trying their hands at every instrument they could get their hands on. They were saints; that's the only explanation I can think of.

Dad's best move was buying me a keyboard with preset songs on it. All you had to do was push a button and the keyboard played *for* you! I remember walking downstairs one Christmas morning to Dad sitting behind the keyboard, bopping up and down, pretending to play "House of the Rising Sun." We may not have had any musical ability, but that wouldn't stop us Fords from having stage presence!

I'm still playing for a living too—just not musical instruments. I'm still delegating, finding creative solutions, managing, problem-solving—just like I did at Michael R. Ford Elementary. Designing is my favorite creative outlet these days. And let me tell ya, designing is a *lot* of problem-solving. I'd say it's at least *50 percent* problem-solving, especially when you're dealing with old houses. I'm not designing everything from scratch. I see situations and problems, and I'm always thinking: *How do I adjust it? How do I fix it? What can I keep? What has to go?* And yes, while problem-solving can absolutely be draining, some of my favorite designs were inspired by problems.

These creative problem-solving skills are skills I picked up along the way while playing. Acting out all of those roles in the Michael R. Ford Elementary School is probably what prepared me to become a CEO. Sound crazy?

Play—imaginary or with objects; or dirt and wood, in Steve's case—helps kids develop problem-solving strategies at an early age; it allows kids to think about their toys, or their structures, or their imaginary friends and figure out how to solve problems. The more we give kids space to problem-solve on their own (with guidance if they need it, of course), the more they'll be able to use their minds creatively.

In 2010, IBM interviewed more than fifteen hundred CEOs, asking them what makes a great leader. Sixty percent of participants said creativity.[1]

Creativity.

The word *creative* comes from the Latin word *creare*, which means "to bring forth." There's a lot of talk about how to be creative, about being creative as a career, as a lifestyle, as a brag-worthy attribute. But here's the thing about it: creativity is not something you can buy or something you can workshop; you either have creativity in you or you don't. And both are fine! But don't fight it either way. If you're a more analytical thinker, then great! We need you in this world. Don't try to start making flower crowns 'cause it's all the rage. If you're naturally creative, then great! We need more of you too! Get creating. You won't be satisfied sitting at a desk in a job that doesn't thrill you.

Creativity doesn't necessarily mean using a glue gun. (Though knowing how to use a glue gun is very useful, thank you very much.) Being creative in the workplace is about coming up with groundbreaking ideas. It's about taking risks. It's about originality.

In his book *Originals*, Adam Grant explains that limiting rules allows children to think for themselves.[2] Additionally, he quotes Teresa Amabile, a Harvard psychologist, who stated in her extensive research on creativity that in one study, parents who limited rules tended to "place emphasis on moral values, rather than on specific rules."[3] Of course, when I read this, it reminded me of our parents. They were much less about rules than they were about focusing on what was right and what was wrong.

While Mom and Dad didn't necessarily have a ton of specific rules, they were strict on the important stuff. When Mom was really upset about something, she'd send us letters on big yellow legal pad paper. She wanted to make sure she covered everything. All of it.

Why letters? She said it was because she didn't want to forget anything. "Plus, you kids might talk back and not listen," she said. You can't talk back to a letter.

———

As Michelle mentioned in the foreword, one really important part of our time as kids was our summers at Deer Valley Family Camp. Those summers were among the most influential experiences of our lives. I'd say our order of life importance was faith, family, Deer Valley—it was that formative for us.

———

Every year, on the same week, the family would load up pretty much everything we owned and head to family camp. Bikes, fishing poles, bedding, towels, clothes for every weather condition—you name it. The only thing we didn't pack was food. Every morning, afternoon, and evening, the dinner bell would ring, and the entire camp would join together to share a meal.

Deer Valley is about two hours south of Pittsburgh, and our family has been going there for nearly forty years. Unlike other families, we didn't go away to summer camp to spend time away from each other—we went to camp to be together as a family.

Here's how a typical day would go: We'd wake up in our cabin and head to the dining hall for breakfast as a family, and then everyone would go their own way. The kids went with their age group and camp counselor for a morning of friend time, and the adults would head to the waterfront to sail, or the craft shop to do ceramics or leather, or go relax with a book.

A couple of hours later, the lunch bell would ring, and the entire camp would meet back together to share a meal. We sat with our families for three meals a day, swapping stories of the adventures we had been on. After lunch it was a free-for-all; everyone would go wherever they wanted and do whatever activity they wanted. Sometimes you did this with your family; sometimes you were free to roam on your own or with your camp friends.

Deer Valley created an amazing sense of independence. There aren't many places on the planet where an eight-year-old is allowed to run off and say, "See ya at the snack bar!" It was this amazing combination of quality family time mixed with independence for a child. And it really shaped who we are.

Steve, Michelle, and I all went on to be camp counselors there over our college summers. Now, that was fun. We still go there with our family to this day. We have started the tradition for the third generation of our family. And this summer we will take our newborn there, the same way I went for the first time when I was barely a year old.

Steve

At summer camp, Dad befriended all the camp counselors. They all loved him. He had a really boisterous personality, and he loved to connect with people. Being at camp was his time to shine and be a kid again. He participated in every activity he could. He was very funny. People really wanted to be around him. Even the counselors wanted to hang out with him!

It was nice to see him relaxed. Dad was such a hard worker, but he'd get there and wouldn't think about work or responsibilities.

Dad would invent all sorts of ridiculous games that everyone wanted to play, like "cross-country bocce ball." There was a bocce court—but that wasn't enough for Dad. He took the bocce ball out of the court, and we'd play across the entire camp. He would chuck the ball as far as he could.

Deer Valley Family Camp was definitely a big part of our lives. Yes, we went there as a family, but it was one of my first introductions to freedom. Sure, I had the woods, but that was just across the street. Deer Valley was different—new people, new territory, and 742 acres to explore. And a lake!

The summer of my senior year was the first time I was going to be a camp counselor and be away from home for the entire summer. It would be my first taste of real independence without being under my parents' watchful eyes.

I felt comfortable around the folks at Deer Valley, like I could be myself. People looked out for me there. Plus, Dad thought it was a good place for me to spread my wings a little bit before college. The job of camp counselor would give me some confidence, but it would force me to take on some responsibility in a safe space. "If Steve's going to mess up, let's let him mess up here," Dad told the camp director, "not at school." I thought it was pretty cool that he saw my being a camp counselor as a way to learn some life lessons before I got to college. It eased me into being independent and learning how to get by without Mom and Dad (though not entirely!). I highly recommend camp for any kid.

Leanne

Outside of playing like pioneer kids, we were pretty traditional. Mom always had dinner on the table at 6:00 on the dot every night. I was in charge of clearing off and setting the table. She wasn't a culinary whiz, but we had food in pretty bowls on matching dishes. And we chatted for a half hour or so—no television. Family time every night—that's not easy to do with three kids. Plus homework. Plus soccer practice. Plus whatever else was going on.

Dad would come home at 5:30 every day. We would hear the garage door open. Mom would put her lipstick on and brush her hair. (Two habits I did *not* inherit from her.) Dad would walk inside wearing his trench coat with his M. R.–initialed briefcase and say, every single day, "Isanybodyhooooome?" And Mom and Dad would give each other a big kiss and hug. We kids would all stop what we were doing to go greet him.

Mom was very traditional, yet she had no problem bending the rules. Sometimes she would say to me, "Do you want me to pick you up early from school tomorrow? Let's go to Pizza Hut." My answer was always yes.

But certain things were completely off-limits. Like most TV.

Steve

Mom and Dad weren't really television fans overall. We were only allowed one hour a day of television, so we *had* to come up with other ways to entertain ourselves. This was a huge part of our upbringing—to create our own entertainment.

Leanne

There are plenty of kids who grew up in this kind of supportive environment, but not everyone is lucky enough to share the creative experiences with their brothers and sisters, let alone grow up to have a TV show together. What's interesting to me is that both Steve and I spent time creating our own worlds. We were using items around the house or outside; we were using our imaginations.

The number one thing that was important to my parents was that we were happy and satisfied in what we were doing. Not what everyone else was doing—what *we* were doing.

All those hours Steve spent playing in the woods and all those hours I spent creating Michael R. Ford Elementary School were crucial to our development and growth, and now, our careers. Sometimes you can make a skateboarding ramp out of bricks. Sometimes you can make an overhead projector out of a car visor mirror.

Steve

Sometimes being raised in a family like ours and having the confidence to do things a bit differently means you don't exactly fit in with the crowd; you're often in the minority. It took me some time to realize that truly creative people and real innovators are pretty much always in the minority. And at the end of the day, that's a pretty great place to be! After all, who wants to be just one of the crowd?

This perspective made things a little tough for me at school while I was growing up. I was a small kid. I know this might be hard to believe because I'm six foot five now. But I was smaller and had buck teeth. I was a late bloomer. I didn't grow until I was a junior in high school. Then—*boom*. I was suddenly six foot five and super skinny.

I had my small group of close friends, but I wasn't in the cool group of kids. At that age, you think being cool matters, but it doesn't.

Apart from shop class, where I was in my element, school was always a bit of a struggle for me. I had a lot of tutors, which was the *worst*.

Throughout school, I was bullied a lot. My first memories of bullying were at elementary school, in first grade. I was on the parallel bars, and a kid punched me in the face. My nose bled. You don't forget these kinds of things; these are the details that stay with you.

Bullying can be cyclical. Once you're picked on and other kids see it, it's more common for the abuse to happen again. It's called a *bullying cycle*.[4]

The worst bullying incident by far was on the school bus. I was in second grade. I was sitting on the bus, minding my own business. A kid— let's call him Jimmy—walked down the aisle of the bus, approached my seat, and spit on me.

I didn't see it coming. I couldn't ever anticipate anyone would do that unprovoked.

That night, Dad went over to Jimmy's house to talk to his father, but Jimmy's father wasn't home. His mother answered the door.

"Jimmy spit on Steve," Dad said.

"That's not the truth," Jimmy's mother responded.

"That *is* the truth," Dad said.

"Well," Jimmy's mother said, "there are many versions of the truth."

Parents often find it difficult to accept that their child is guilty of bullying. But I had witnesses who backed me up. I had friends who were on the school bus that day, and they spoke to the principal. It helps to have a friend stick their neck out for you and tell an adult.

Jimmy got suspended for a day.

People today think that cyberbullying has taken the place of face-to-face bullying, but it hasn't. In fact, 19 percent of kids in high school across the country were reported to have been bullied on school property in 2017.[5] That's almost one in five. And those are the kids who will admit to it. Being bullied is humiliating—not something that someone wants to admit to. In fact, I feel pretty uncomfortable talking about it in this book, but I'm doing it because I think it's so important for kids and parents to talk to each other about it.

After the bus incident, Dad bought a punching bag and soft boxing gloves. He took me down to the basement and showed me how to hit the punching bag. The next thing I knew, I was training. Dad and I would fake fight each other often. I was small then—only in the second grade—so Dad would get on his knees to train me.

Sometimes we would play-fight, like a game. Dad would lie on his back and wiggle his knees. I would fall on top of him; then he'd chase me and my sisters around the house. He'd call himself "mad dog," and he would crawl around barking, "Mad dog! Mad dog! Ruff, ruff, ruff!" It was the best.

One night, Mom was out of town and Dad was home with the three of us. He and I were boxing each other. He was down on his knees, and I swung at him with these giant gloves on and missed. But because he was at my level, and because I have pretty big teeth, my mouth went right into his cheek, and I accidentally bit him. He had to go to the hospital to get stitches. He never made me feel bad about it once. Dad was such a great guy.

We kept training. Dad never wanted me to start a fight, but he didn't want me to get bullied either. "It's okay to defend yourself," he said.

More bullying went on in the seventh and eighth grades, but I was fighting back. For some reason, the school decided to punish me along with the bully—it didn't matter who started the fight. I had to go to in-school suspension in the principal's office. Our school had a little room with a desk and a window in the door, like a jail cell. I had to do my work there all day. Mom remembers me being indignant about it: I didn't start the fight; why did I have to be punished like the aggressor? It wasn't fair.

By high school, the teachers knew I wasn't instigating these fights. So anytime a fight in school happened, the teachers had my back. The best part of being in a fight in school is that you know it's only going to last for a few minutes. You're always waiting for the teacher to show up. I would look over my shoulder, just waiting for the teacher to come over and stop things.

My parents really didn't know about the bullying in high school because I kept it to myself. In a way, I guess I had resigned myself to it. I never really complained, and I never refused to go to school. I soldiered on.

Michelle knew about it, though, and she felt really bad for me. For a little while, she thought maybe if I tried to fit in a little more, the bullying would stop. But I needed to follow my own path. I wasn't a follower; I acted how I wanted to act.

Michelle says now that she thinks I was brave then because I didn't cave in to these kids. But I was just being myself. I was being goofy. I wasn't worried about my hair or my clothes. Sometimes that's what you get when you're an individual. You can get picked on for that. The world wants you to be in one box—and I wasn't going to go in that box.

Leanne

Some people *do* get nervous when they see someone being true to themselves. That happens with guys in a physical bullying way. And it can happen with girls in a mean-girl way. I had my own issues with some mean girls.

I had to find new friends in middle school because my old friends were being mean to everyone—including me. It was seventh grade, and these girls were insecure about themselves; they didn't want to be made fun of. So they turned it around and made fun of everyone else. It was so messed up. I didn't want to join in on that. I'm thankful I saw what was happening and had the guts and the confidence to get away from them. That's not easy to do in seventh grade.

But my experience was nothing like what Steve went through.

Steve

During high school, there was a guy—let's call him Joe—who *hated* my haircut. I mean, Joe was relentless. He picked on me for what felt like forever. Joe sat behind me in English class and constantly harassed me, called me names, because of my long hair. I don't want to remember the names I was called. Trust me: whatever he said, it was mean.

Joe and I ended up going to the same college. I saw him at a party my freshman year. And—what do you know?—Joe had grown his hair out. He had the same haircut as me—the one I had in high school that he made fun of me for.

I didn't want to make a big deal about it, because that's not how I am. I'm not a spiteful guy. I'm not looking for revenge. But I had to say *something* after getting tormented over my hair for an entire year. Now this guy had the same haircut?

So I walked up to Joe and said, "Cool hair."

Once I grew up and went to college, the bullying stopped. By then, I was as tall as I am now and knew how to fight. No one wanted to fight me anymore. But the bullying I went through as a kid was stressful. It was memorable—the kind of memories you want to erase. Kids who are bullied can feel depressed and experience anxiety. They can do poorly in school, stop eating, stop sleeping.

I didn't understand it then, but now I do. Bullies bully because they're unhappy and don't like themselves, so they need to make other people feel bad in order to get through the day. This is the way I look at it now: I feel bad for those kids. That's the truth.

Leanne

I hate it that both of us went through this—especially Steve, because it was so prolonged—but I'm grateful that both of us had the strength to stay true to who we are. Really, what impresses me about Steve's reaction is his compassion. He has empathy for his bullies! It's not an easy thing to do, to look at someone's life, even as they're hurting you, and feel empathy for them. But as with any challenge, going through those experiences gave us the very strength that has helped us get where we are now. It's the hard times along the way that make us so grateful for who we have become.

WORKING ON PROGRESS

How can we encourage children to stay young and enjoy their youth?

How can we play more with our children? Laugh more? Create more?

How can we encourage children to use their imaginations more? To turn off the TV, turn off the video games? Can we lead by example?

Can we make a conscious effort to get off our phones and get outside and play?

As an adult, what do you still do that feels like playing? Does it create a better, happier life for you? Can you do that more often?

3

Dead Broke and Filthy Rich

Don't ask yourself what the world needs. Ask yourself
what makes you come alive and then go do that. Because
what the world needs is people who have come alive.

–HOWARD THURMAN

Leanne

Dad had a saying: "Don't major in the minors." He was a big-picture
thinker. He believed that we should look at the overall view of life, that
the choices we make should work toward a greater goal. (Yes, this can
even apply to decorating. When I'm telling someone to make a change
in their house that they're uncomfortable with, I'll think to myself and

then remind them: "Don't major in the minors. Does your choice suit the greater good of your house? Look at the bigger picture.")

Though he'd say it often when we were growing up, college was probably the first time Dad's favorite motto really registered with me.

I went to Ohio University. It was a beautiful, tree-lined college with brick roads and brick buildings. I wanted to live the life of an artist. Early on I knew this. But I also wanted to be an artist who was business savvy. I was thrilled when I found out about the bachelor of specialized studies program. It allowed me to create my own degree program, one that was tailored to what I needed to learn to follow the path toward what I wanted to do. You literally make your own curriculum. I decided on the classes I wanted to take, then wrote up a syllabus and explanation for why. I named my major *integrated retail communications*.

I took all the advertising, public relations, graphic design, art, and retail classes I could find. I designed my own line of clothing, MessAndMod ("messed with and modified clothing"), and I treated it as if it were a business. I created a catalog and a fashion show concept. I even made a website for it with the help of a friend. And let me tell you this: making a website was *very* ahead of its time, considering we were still listening to all our music on Napster.

I was into it! And I was motivated! I was in charge of creating my own path. This program was a huge platform and jumping-off point for me.

A lot of people go to college and take the kinds of classes that make their parents happy. They take the classes they think they're supposed to take. Or they think, *Is this what's going to make me the most money?* And maybe that works for them; maybe that's what they want. But a better question would be: Is it going to make *you* happy? Otherwise it will be a short-lived career, I'll tell ya that.

I remember my girlfriends in college being so stressed out when they were trying to figure out their majors. I remember thinking, *You're eighteen years old! Pick something you love deeply. (It's probably going to change anyway.)*

I didn't have a clear path either, by the way. I was excited to learn. I was excited to create. Your brain doesn't necessarily have to color within the lines that life has told you to stay in. It doesn't have to be this clean little zone. Your passion can look different than you expected, different than what you started with.

So many people have asked me how I got into interior design and what I went to school for. I went into college thinking I was studying public relations! (And then had many other zigs and zags, which—don't you worry—you will hear all about.) I'm very quick to tell people I *did not* go to school for design. Would some of those skills have helped me if I had? Absolutely. But they're not always necessary.

What you *do* need is grit and experience.

Experience is crucial, so I added the requirement of an internship to my school curriculum. I knew I needed field work—hands-on experience. And I knew I wanted to be in New York. I knew I wanted to be in fashion, even if it seemed incredibly unrealistic. I started applying for internships.

A lot of creative jobs pay very little, by the way. On the outside, creative jobs often look like glamour jobs because of the clothes, because of the location, because of the type of people surrounding them. But it seems that the reality is that the more creative the job is, the less glamorous it actually is.

I called my parents, as one does when one needs some sound advice.

"Dad, I'm going to get into pharmaceutical sales. They make $100,000 out of the gate," I said. "I'll just buy cool clothes instead of make them."

But my father didn't flinch.

"Don't major in the minors," Dad said. "Think big picture. That is not what you went to school to do. This is a temporary problem, Leanne. In twenty years, do you want to be the head of a pharmaceutical sales company?"

In other words, make sure that when you get to the top of the corporate ladder, you don't look down, and look over, and say, "Oh shoot. Wrong ladder."

Steve

When I was in my twenties, I wanted to snowboard all the time. So I came up with a plan that I thought was a great idea: become a ski patroller.

I started at my local resort, Seven Springs Mountain Resort. I got a winter job there as a ski patroller while I was still in school. I thought it was perfect: I could ski patrol (which by the way, is a very hard job) and also snowboard. It would keep me on the mountain, which is what I wanted, because I loved being outside.

But being a ski patroller isn't necessarily the kind of job you want to have in your forties because—I'm not going to lie—it's difficult to make money in that profession. It would be difficult to contribute to a family. Getting a management job at a ski resort seemed like the perfect job for me. But from what I saw, only a handful of people are able to do that. Plus, I was getting pressure from my family at the time not to be a ski bum. "Go get a job," they told me. The big picture was getting harder and harder to envision.

Dad, like any good parent, wanted me to focus on a stable career, the kind of career that would help me afford to pay for the extreme sports that I loved, because that gear isn't cheap.

I was trying to make snowboarding into more than just a sport that I loved. I was trying to build my life around it, which wasn't easy.

Though there was a time that I loved being a ski patroller, I slowly started getting burned-out. Being a ski patroller took the fun out of snowboarding for me. It took away the novelty of it because I was on the mountain every day, working very hard. In fact, I stopped snowboarding for a long time because of that experience.

Now I've turned something else that I love to do—carpentry—into a career. It took me a little while, but I kept striving toward the big picture. I don't like sitting at a desk. I love construction work, as long as it's creative. Of course, if you do anything long enough, it becomes a job.

Leanne

It's worth noting here that Steve graduated with a degree in recreation. Yep. It's just too perfect. Steve went to school to become a professional vacationer.

Steve

Leanne loves that joke. That's exactly the reason I went for my degree in parks and recreation, because I knew I wanted to be outside! I knew that would make me happy, breathing in the fresh air. I even took it a step further; I bet you don't know this, Leanne, but when I applied to colleges, I purposely applied to West Virginia University for two reasons. The first was the parks and recreation major. But the other reason was because WVU also happened to be fifty-three minutes from Ohiopyle, Pennsylvania, which was one of the best places to white-water kayak in the area. It wasn't that I wanted to skip out on school and be a full-time kayaker. (Okay, of course I did!) I graduated college, but having that outlet made school less painful to me.

I scheduled my classes two days a week so that I could kayak. I also worked at Immersion Research, a white-water rafting clothing company, three days a week. I got myself a job making clothes. My first job there was to hand stamp grommets on their shorts.

A huge part of focusing on the big picture is finding out what you truly love to do and then doing it. The world doesn't need people walking through life like zombies, making choices about their lives just because it seems like what they should do. Life is short, so make it worthwhile and do what makes you feel the happiest and most fulfilled.

So while most college students arrange their lives around their class schedules and football games, I arranged my life around getting to the river.

Kayaking helped me build confidence. It was an adrenaline rush, and it introduced me to a new group of friends, many of whom are still friends to this day.

My parents had always encouraged me to play traditional sports, like baseball or basketball. But traditional sports weren't my thing; I was more into rock climbing, skiing, and mountain biking. My dad had played basketball and baseball as a kid, so he was a bit crushed that I wasn't interested in following in his footsteps. But I always appreciated that he wanted to help me find my own thing that inspired me.

And I did start to figure out what inspired me by the time I got to high school, though it wasn't exactly something that my parents were all too happy about. My parents knew the risks involved in extreme sports.

I would hang out in this store called Mountain Dreams that sold knives and gear and backpacks. The kind of place you could really get lost in if you loved camping and outdoor gear like I did. Occasionally, I'd drag my parents in there, and we found out they had rock-climbing classes. I had already started talking to my parents about rock climbing because of how much time I spent at Mountain Dreams.

"If you're going to rock climb," Dad said, "let's put you in a rock-climbing class so you can learn how to do it safely." I'm sure they thought, *Couldn't he have been easier and just picked up a baseball bat?* But they were always so supportive, so they sent me to rock-climbing school. Their thinking was this: *We're going to help you figure this out because we don't want you to die.*

Once I learned the basics of rock climbing, I got hooked. Some buddies and I started rappelling and free climbing on anything we could find over a few stories tall, including churches, towers, and bridges—basically, anything that had a roof. I also went to plenty of parks, like Cooper's Rock State Forest and Seneca Rocks State Park in West Virginia—both fantastic places to climb. At Mount Davis, which is the highest point in Pennsylvania, we used to climb on the fire tower, where you could see five states from the top. My friends and I would climb up this one-hundred-foot-tall fire tower and rappel down.

In my town, we were a little more limited. When you're in the city or the suburbs, and you don't feel like driving over an hour just to climb, you climb whatever is nearby. On a school night, I couldn't exactly head over to Seneca Rocks, so we'd find structures to climb. (All of this is very illegal, by the way. Kids, you should not try this at home!) As crazy as this sounds, I was very safe about it. The only time I felt scared was when we were climbing up the side of one of those old churches with big stones. We were doing what's called "bouldering," where you climb horizontally along a rock without any ropes. You scale it low because you're going in a horizontal direction. If you climb above a certain height, you could really get hurt.

I accidentally climbed vertically—I guess I didn't realize how far up

I was because it was at night. Suddenly, I was too far up the side of the church to jump down. I had to make a decision to go up or down, and I was close enough to the roof that I decided to climb up. I ended up getting stuck on the roof of this church, which was not the plan. (Mom, I'm sorry!) Luckily, my climbing gear was in the car, so my buddy threw me a rope, and I rappelled about forty feet back down.

Rock climbing was just my first taste of extreme sports. Soon, I propelled myself into the next sport that would change my life: white-water kayaking.

I first saw people white-water kayaking when I was on a white-water rafting trip around the age of thirteen. The kayakers traveled down the river, cruising over waterfalls and bobbing in and out on the rapids. I thought, *Well, that looks more fun than what I'm doing here, which is just sitting in a raft.*

By the time I was seventeen, my friend and I made a pact that we were going to learn to kayak together. We decided to save money to make our dream a reality. I wrote down my goal of how much I was going to save, and I put a date on that goal. I knew that if I was going to accomplish something, I needed it in black and white. I was going to buy a kayak. I needed to save $500 so I could make that happen.

And that's exactly what I did. I saved $500 working as a camp counselor. I was so thrilled. A couple of weeks later at the end of summer, I was ready to buy a kayak. I was pumped up.

"Let's go buy these kayaks and get this going," I said to my friend.

He gave me a confused look. "I don't have any money," he said.

"We made this goal to buy kayaks," I said. "What did you do with all of your money?"

"Uh, what money?"

Needless to say, my friend didn't save his money.

But I did. Nothing was stopping me from getting that kayak.

I drove down to Ohiopyle, Pennsylvania, which is a great rafting town on the Youghiogheny River, with a number of rushing waterfalls, and went to the kayaking store.

"I'd like to buy a kayak," I said. "I know nothing about kayaking. What do I need?" I had $500 in my pocket, and I bought all the gear I'd need: kayak, life jacket, helmet, paddle.

I drove down to a launching spot next to the river, got in my kayak—and I just sat there. I didn't know a thing about kayaking! These were intense white-water rapids at Ohiopyle. One of the falls is an eighteen-foot drop that was off-limits most of the year. The waterfalls at Ohiopyle are no joke. I could have drowned.

A few guys came up to the launch area, and I happened to know one of them. So I figured I'd just put it out there and ask for some help.

"Can I go down the river with you?" I said.

"Sure, come on," he answered.

Next thing I knew, I was going down the river with this group of guys. It was awesome and just felt very natural. Frightening too! I was out of my element for the first time, and of course, I had fears of getting hurt or drowning. But I went for it. I threw myself into that river and paddled my heart out.

Somehow I ended up having this ability that I didn't even know I had. All the guys I was with ended up "swimming," or falling out of their kayaks. See, the white-water kayaks have what's called a skirt that goes around your waist and seals the lower half of your body if you flip over. You can release the skirt and let yourself out to swim if you roll over and can't get back up. It's fun to swim if it's summertime and the water is seventy degrees, but you're likely to hit the rocks or suck in water. It's all great fun until you smash your head into a rock or get scraped on the bottom of the river. I didn't need to do that, though—I didn't fall out of my kayak once.

We had an incredible day on the river. Later, we drank beer and hung out by the fire all night. I thought, *I want to do this every day.*

In many ways, white-water kayaking sparked something in me. It was the ability to set a goal and achieve it. This sport, which was something I had never done before, was a challenge. I wanted to figure it out, and I did. It was the first time I really took initiative in something that I loved, and it was a good feeling. Yes, I took count-less spills and took my beatings on the rocks, but I figured it out (and never lost my teeth!).

White-water kayaking is an extreme sport that gets you into nature and challenges you—physically and mentally. I did it, and I was a bet-ter person because of that. Sometimes you need to have some grit to achieve a goal. I knew that if I could take on this challenge, I could do anything I set my mind to.

Leanne

Steve tried to teach me to kayak. And it was all great until the first time I flipped over. I'd call it more terrifying than fun.

Steve

It can be terrifying! Don't get me wrong. There were some hairy expe-riences too.

That winter, I went with friends who were really experienced kay-akers. Up until that point, I had been doing well, and I was probably overconfident. There was snow on the ground and ice in the water, and I didn't have the appropriate gear yet. Everyone else was wearing long underwear and waterproof dry suits; I was wearing a rain suit. I didn't have the money to buy a real dry suit. And everyone was a little concerned.

"I'm not going to come out of my kayak," I insisted. "I'm not going to swim. I'm going to be fine." Again, I was a little overconfident . . . Okay, *very* overconfident.

The snow melt really affects the water level and what the river looks like; it can be completely different from one day to the next. I made it through every rapid, but just as I was going down the river in a choppy area, I flipped over. This is normal in kayaking, but this time I couldn't get back up. I'd roll over, come up for air, and then roll over again. I kept missing my opportunity to get back upright. Three times in a row: I missed it. I missed it. I missed it.

I couldn't zip myself out of the skirt because if I was in that freezing water, I would be in a lot of trouble. Hypothermia could set in in fewer than fifteen minutes.

I saw that there was a guy close to me, so I did what's called a bow rescue, hoping to get his attention. I smacked my hands on the bottom of the kayak until he saw me, and then I was able to grab onto his kayak to lift myself up.

That experience taught me a lot—especially to have the right gear.

I had other treacherous moments kayaking, but I wouldn't give up any of it. That's how much I love the sport.

With kayaking, I went down to that river and said to myself, *I'm going to learn how to kayak today*. I took control of what I wanted out of life. Things worked out for me, I believe, because I was following an interest that propelled me. I arranged my life around what I loved. I had the confidence to go for it.

You can apply this to anything, really. It's about being an active participant in your own life.

Even though I don't make a living in extreme sports, both snow-boarding and kayaking have become hobbies that I really enjoy again. They are a big part of what makes my life richer—what makes my life more than about working and doing what it takes to earn a living.

It was important to me to focus on those sports instead of taking a straight career path. I was much more focused on the "recreation" aspect of my life—not too far from my college degree! Which worked for me.

Not everyone knows exactly what they want in college or right out of college. I knew I liked to be outside. I knew I liked to be active. Not everyone is able to find themselves so quickly, like Leanne was able to. And I commend her for it! She has amazing drive and has always known what she wanted out of life. I did too—but it looked a little different. To be honest, I wanted to extend my childhood as long as I could. (Have you ever heard of Peter Pan syndrome?) So, while I didn't totally follow Dad's advice, it was something that was always in the back of my mind. I got there eventually; it just took a bit longer for me than most people.

WORKING ON PROGRESS

What's the big-picture plan for your life?

What small details are stopping you from thinking about the big picture?

What small steps can you take to get going in the right direction?

What path are you on? Is it the right path, or do you need to take a few steps backward to get cruising on?

4

Show Up Anyway

Find out who you are and do it on purpose.

—DOLLY PARTON

Leanne

I have one main piece of advice when it comes to life. If you already get this concept, then you can put this book down. I have nothing to say that you don't already know. It's this simple rule: *show up*. You want to be an interior designer? Show up and design. You want to be a singer? Show up and sing. Are you a parent? Show up for your kids.

And honestly, you can stop reading now. That's the point. That's the climax. The denouement. The happy ending.

It's amazing what can happen to you just by getting out of bed, getting off the couch, getting off the phone, and showing up.

Steve

When I was in college, I'd have to sit in front of the class. I'd have to know my professor's name. I'd have to make sure that I stopped in after class to find out when there was a tutoring session—then actually go to the tutoring session. Showing up was a big part of my education. If I wasn't passing, or if I was struggling, then meeting with a professor or a teacher in high school would go a long way. If I showed up after class and said, "Hey, I need some help," it sent the message that I was trying. Somewhere, someone wise—or maybe someone not so wise?—said, "Eighty percent of success is showing up."

Showing up isn't just about being there. It's also about bringing your *mind* to it. It's about getting involved in what you want to do. You can just show up somewhere and be a stump on a log—but that's not what I'm talking about.

Leanne

Really showing up means finding and then following your passion—figuring out what makes you happy to get out of your very cozy bed each morning. This can be career, family, art, hobbies—you name it. But we all need to find that "it" that makes us come alive. Once you do, you will find it's contagious to those around you. Soon, others will notice that they need to get excited in life and "come alive." It's wildfire. And it's fun.

Life is tough, really tough. There is sadness, heartbreak, stress, and anxiety. Isn't that an even better reason to get your kicks where you can? There's so much hate and sorrow and sadness in the world that we need to add more love. What if we can dilute all the hate by pouring in extra love and joy?

———————

While Steve was kayaking, I was in Ohio, and I knew I needed to get to New York if I wanted to start my fashion career. So I decided to move to New York City for the summer and get an internship in fashion. I couldn't believe my luck when I landed an internship at one of my favorite brands, Betsey Johnson. Now, the gig at Betsey Johnson was short-lived, and we'll talk more about that later, but for now, suffice it to say I was willing to pick up and go to where the action was to get what I wanted in life. (Still am.)

I've always loved fashion and clothing design. When I was younger, I made my own clothes. Yes, I was crafty (remember: my sister did call me "pioneer lady"), and I liked making my own clothes. But the real reason I was making my own clothes and digging through piles at Goodwill was because I had no money. I had to get creative out of necessity! In my early twenties, I used to run around in what I swear to you were drapes. As in, the drapes were nailed up to the wall in my little room.

All that to say, on the quest to finding what I loved, I just knew that I had to get to New York. I had to *show up*.

Last night, Courtney from my design team reminded me of how we met. She messaged me online and asked to take me to coffee. I didn't have time for coffee, but I told her that we were installing a house that week for the show and that she should come by to help. Guess what? She showed up, not knowing what she was getting into, and with no real knowledge or background of interiors. She showed up with a desire to learn and a readiness to work hard. She went from offering free labor, to being paid hourly, to having a full-time role at Leanne Ford Interiors! And I now consider Courtney my principal interior stylist, which means she oversees and styles the props, foliage, and details for all of my interior projects. She works with the interiors photographers to create incredible images. Her career has taken an unexpected turn, and she now has a portfolio of fifteen projects that can get her work anywhere in the world. All because she showed up.

Back in 2002, I was closing up my senior year of college. It was less than a year after my first quick stint in New York for the internship at Betsey Johnson. I was looking through old fashion magazines at a used bookstore. My friend Meg had a crush on the guy who worked there, so we went often to stalk—I mean, *visit*—him. While she flirted, I flipped through an old *W* magazine. I saw this tiny article with a tiny picture about a company called Heatherette. In the picture, there were two guys dancing down a checkered runway. One was dressed as a cowboy, and one was dressed as a sailor. Glitter everywhere. They looked so happy.

I wanted to be surrounded by people who loved their work. I had to figure out my next move. When I saw that photo, something clicked. I thought, *That's what I love about fashion. That's who I want to work with. People who love their jobs.* I know that sounds crazy, to decide that you're going to focus on a company that you know nothing about. But that didn't even cross my mind.

I had always made my own clothing. I cut shirts, spray-painted them, Sharpied them, sewed mix-and-match shirts together. Friendly reminder: this was 2003, so don't judge me. It was (almost) totally acceptable. Our college was in a small town with a limited number of shops to buy from—one, to be exact. All the girls walked around in matching outfits. We didn't have much choice. But if you ask me, it was nothing a Sharpie couldn't fix! My favorite shirt had *ROCK ON* in huge iron-on letters on the front, and I wrote on the back: "If music be the food of love, play on. Give me excess of it."[1] (Yep, a Shakespeare quote; I'm such a romantic.) Only, I crossed out *play on* and wrote *ROCK ON* over it.

I am smiling just writing this. Sums me up perfectly.

I even made my boyfriends' shirts. (Sorry for the plural *boyfriends*, but hey, I was young. And they were all just so darn cute!) My favorite was *Pancho Lives* in massive iron-on letters. It's a reference to one of my favorite songs, "Pancho and Lefty," by Townes Van Zandt. I'd like to think that guy is still wearing that T-shirt out there somewhere today.

Anyway, I found a contact number for Heatherette. Now, this was pre-Google, by the way. It wasn't easy to find a contact number, but I was determined. I got on my roommate's massive computer, started that dial-up internet, and found their website, which pretty much looked like an Atari screen. But there was a contact number. So I called them.

The phone rang a few times, and the call went to voice mail.

"Welcome to Heatherette trailer park," the twangy voice mail said. "Leave a message."

I kid you not. Did I leave a message? *(Twangy voice)* You bet I did.

"Hey there. This is Leanne Ford," I said. "I just saw your picture dancing down a checkered runway and, well, I want to come help you! Call me back!"

Knowing what I know *now*, I should have said, "OH YEAH! FOR FREE!" if I really wanted to get a call back.

Heatherette was a kitschy, club-kid, punk-inspired collection that was just gaining momentum. Paris Hilton and Boy George were a staple at their runway shows, sometimes modeling, sometimes hanging out. It felt like a younger, fresher version of Betsey Johnson. (I know. A one-eighty from what I like now—all black and white.) It was started by former ice skater and club kid Richie Rich and former cowboy Traver Rains. They handmade their own stuff. Just like me! I was into it.

Not surprisingly, the guys from Heatherette didn't call me back.

That was fine. When they didn't call back, I left another message. And when they didn't call back again, I emailed them.

I was fearless verging on oblivious—and why not? Not a thing to lose. I had made a ton of clothes too! I had just created my own line of clothing for my major in college. I had a website with photos of my handmade "special" clothes, all those pieces that I had made and cut up and spray-painted.

"I'd love to come work for you," I wrote in my email, and I sent them a link to my website.

I could have sat there thinking, *I have no chance. I'm this little young chick sitting in Ohio. I have no business making these random calls.* But you never know if you never try!

I finally got an email back. I was astounded. Thrilled. It read: "Hey, we have a fashion show in two weeks if you want to come help."

I wrote back: "I'll be there."

I didn't say, "How will I get there?" I didn't say, "Can you reimburse my flight?" I simply said, "I'll be there." There are risks in life that you have to take; sometimes the stakes are so high that you can't complicate it with details.

I'll be there.

Reminder: I wasn't living in New York at the time—I had come back to Ohio after being in the city for only a month. It was time to finish college! I didn't want the guys from Heatherette dealing with the logistics, if even just mentally. Instead, I took on that responsibility. I wanted this experience. I would have done anything to see a fashion show up close and personal, so I was determined to figure it out on my own.

This is a major piece of advice that I often tell people looking to get hired: don't tell people that you're from anywhere except where they need you to be.

Your answer should always be "I'll be there."

I did this throughout my career, actually, no matter where I lived: Nashville, Los Angeles, Pittsburgh. If someone asked me to do a job, I simply showed up.

I called my parents and said, "I'm flying back to New York to help on a fashion show." I'm sure my jumping all over the place stressed them out. But they knew I was a creative soul, and taking chances was part of my DNA. Plus, I was going to stay for the weekend with a friend who was a New York City police officer. I was safe and sound. They gave me the okay.

The Heatherette fashion show was wild. Okay, that's an understatement. It was like a rave: glitter, electronic music, psychedelic lights, club kids everywhere.

I was wearing an outfit that I'd made myself. It was a skirt that I wore as a long tube top. I used the bottom of a T-shirt I had cut off as a type of belt over it. (As I write this, I'm wondering how I even came up with this outfit. I'm slightly confused and completely entertained by my younger self.)

By the end of the night, I was talking to one of the male models. One of the only straight men there seemed to have a little crush on me— little Ohio me! Noticing this flirtation, the Heatherette guys, Richie and Traver, asked me to come out with them after the fashion show. Yes, please! We went out—as a small group, maybe five of us—and stayed out until the papers came out at 6:00 a.m. They wanted to wait for the *New York Times* review of the show.

I was running around New York with Richie and Traver, these sweet designers who were so welcoming, so lovely, so inspiring and alive, and we were waiting for the morning paper to read the reviews of the fashion show I'd just helped with. I was in my glory.

That's when I finally told them that I actually lived in Ohio.

"Ohio? If we had known you were in Ohio, we wouldn't have asked you to come; that's so far away for you!"

"That's why I didn't tell you!" I said with a wink.

Fast-forward to 6:00 a.m. The reviews came out: the show was a success. I can remember it perfectly. We were all celebrating and dancing in the streets with our papers at dawn.

"Can I come intern for you?" I asked Richie. "I gotta come back and work for you."

"Come over whenever you want, honey bunny," Richie said.

See you there.

After I graduated college early, my two friends drove me to NYC in a two-door Chevrolet Cavalier—the three of us and all of my worldly belongings. (Shout-out to space bags for somehow making everything fit.)

I worked for Heatherette an entire year for free.

How could you afford it? I hear you asking. First of all, I had financial help and support from my parents. Not everyone is lucky enough to have that, and I'm grateful that I did. This kind of help can't be underestimated.

I spoke to my parents about the situation. I told them that I wanted to move to Manhattan and that I was interested in interning for Heatherette. I didn't know what their reaction would be. They had been supportive up to this point, but it's an entirely different situation when your daughter calls up to say, "Hi. I'm moving to New York City without any money to work for a couple of crazy designers."

Instead, they gave me the greatest gift to help start my career: financial freedom.

"We've saved for all our kids just in case they wanted to go to graduate school," Dad said. "*This* is your graduate school." They agreed to pay the $800 a month that I needed for rent in Manhattan for the first year.

I was thrilled. Completely overwhelmed and so excited.

"This is big for your career," my parents said.

They could have easily said, "You're going to work for a couple of club kids? We're not paying your rent in New York," and that would have been that. But my parents were committed to it. They knew I was a good kid. They knew I was a self-starter. They knew I had to take this risk. And they knew I had guts.

Look: nothing in life is done without fear. Courage isn't the absence of fear; it's working through the fear. That's what risk-taking is about. If you take a risk, it's not that you won't be nervous—you should be! In fact, prepare to be nervous. If you aren't making anyone nervous, you aren't doing anything special.

For the last year of college, I had worked as a bartender and squirreled away all of my money, which helped me survive in New York. I used all of my savings. I made my own clothes. I had fabric hanging on my wall (as a sort of alternative to wallpaper—a rental survival solution) that I would pull down and wear out as a dress at night. Yes, really. I was Julie Andrews from *The Sound of Music.* I was Scarlett from *Gone with the Wind.* I'd literally wear this fabric out at night, tie it all around me with safety pins and suede rope that I had from summer camp. And at the end of the night, when I came home and got ready for bed, I'd hang the fabric right back up on the wall.

While $800 was (and is) a lot of money, it goes nowhere in Manhattan. I lived right on Restaurant Row, a popular street where people go to eat before they go to the theater. It's a busy street filled with Italian restaurants and steak houses, and I couldn't afford to go to any of them. My room was the size of a bed. I slept under my clothes rack. I ate pita bread and two scrambled eggs three times a day. It was $1.29 a meal.

I continued to make my own clothing, since I certainly couldn't afford to buy anything new! My favorite dress to wear around New

York City was this little minidress (if you could call it that) that I made out of an old '80s prom dress someone gave me. She had worn it for a costume party and was going to throw it away. I cut off the top half and wore the bottom half as a mini baby doll dress. (It was three long layers of peach chiffon—can you blame me?!) It didn't quite fit, so I took a safety pin that had a massive denim flower, glued it and made it work. I wore that dress all summer long—a little "fashion girl" running around the Lower East Side in a chiffon '80s dress.

I did everything for Richie and Traver. When I say everything—I'm not exaggerating. I'd stand in the post office line for two and a half hours. I'd glue glitter on sweatshirts and ship them to Japan. I'd push racks of clothes across Manhattan, sweating and smiling the entire way. I was just so happy to be there. It was incredibly inspiring to be around people who were doing it for themselves. They were getting tons of press, and if you didn't know better, you would think there were a hundred people working for them. They were gurus at marketing. They taught me the power of press and what self-promotion could do. It seemed as though they were a massive company, but it was just us: Richie Rich; Traver Rains; Mackie Dugan, their pattern maker. (I can remember perfectly one night on Bowery when Mackie stole my high heels and taught me the proper way to walk like a lady.) And then there was me. The four of us did it all.

And that was good for a while, real good.

Steve

It was the same for me during those first years away from home. That's how I started everything in my life: I showed up. I also worked really hard. Working at Immersion Research (a paddling-gear manufacturer) three days a week. Taking college classes two days a week. And then on Saturdays and Sundays for two years, I worked at Seven Springs Mountain Resort as a safety ranger. I got a job there so I could afford a lift ticket. (This was a big part of how I was able to afford all of my expensive outdoor hobbies, by the way. Because skiing, rock climbing, snowboarding, and kayaking gear is not cheap. It's *expensive*. Want to snowboard? Get a job on the mountain. Want to kayak? Get a job as a white-water rafting instructor.)

Anyway, part of my job as a safety ranger was to make sure that the mountain was safe for skiing, but there was also a policing element to it, which I didn't love. We had to make sure everyone was buying tickets. If you didn't have a ticket, my job was to call the police on you. And I didn't want to bust people. It seemed hypocritical. (Look: I only had a ski pass because I worked there. If I couldn't afford a ski pass, I would have probably been trying to get on the mountain for free too!) Instead of calling the police, I'd wanted to take people to the ticket booth and make them buy a ticket. But that wasn't the policy; we were supposed to call the cops.

I needed another way to work on the mountain. So I left the safety rangers and joined the ski patrol. It was a big commitment to get on ski patrol. You had to show up in the summer for training, then take all of the necessary exams: how to give first aid, how to ride a toboggan, and how to transport patrol equipment. The first year you had to be a volunteer, and I put a lot of effort into that position. (There were a select few who got paid during the week as well.) I started as a volunteer and eventually got paid for working shifts.

Since it was mostly a volunteer position, I wasn't able to afford the best place to live. But that never bothered me. I didn't need much. There was an abandoned cabin in the middle of the ski slope, and I talked the ski patrol into letting me stay in the cabin during the summer as an employee perk. (In the summer, I worked as a kayak brand represen-tative. In the winter I worked as ski patrol.)

A cabin sounds real nice, right? Leanne lived in a sweet little cabin in Los Angeles that some of you may have heard about.

This cabin wasn't like that.

When I moved in, it was infested with mice. There was water, but it wasn't drinkable water. There was electricity, but maybe just one little light.

Mom hates this story because that cabin was *rough*. I lived in a lot of rough places. I lived in a tent. In my car. In my trailer. To me, this cabin was awesome.

Leanne

It was as if you were playing in the woods all over again!

Steve

It was! To my parents it wasn't as awesome. (None of the places were.) I only ended up living there for a summer. It would have been doable in the winter—and it would have been really cool—but it would have been some hard living.

Ski patrolling was a great job for me for a little while. But there were some stressful moments. People fall on ski slopes, and they get hurt. It was my job to get them down off the mountain for help. Every year at our resort, we had more than twenty-five hundred incident reports that ranged from frostbite to broken bones to cardiac arrest. And a whole lot of head injuries.

The first accident that I remember involved a teenage girl. She had fallen, and I came up on her just sitting in the middle of the trail.

"I fell and hurt my knee," she said. "I can't move my knee or my leg." She wasn't that upset. She was pretty still, actually.

You have to feel for an injury, and her knee felt really weird. Her pants had no zipper up the leg, so I had to cut her ski pant open up to her knee to see what was going on there. I'm going to save you from the gory details, but her knee was completely dislocated. It was bad.

It freaked me out because it was my first accident, but I stayed calm and stabilized her. A ski patroller is not a doctor. You're not going to fix anybody. Your goal is to make the person comfortable, get them to the bottom of the hill, and not add to their pain. The worst-case scenario would be having to give CPR.

"You're going to be fine," I told the girl, trying to be as calm as possible. I didn't want to scare her. I called for a sled, secured her, and gently got her down the hill, where she was transferred to a hospital.

Another memorable "accident"—if you could even call it that—is really funny. I was working, and I got this call that someone was in the ski lodge with an injury.

"Hey, I have an injury," this guy said. He was about nineteen or twenty years old. "I have this splinter in my finger."

A splinter?

"Are you serious?" I said.

Now, this kid was fully an adult. He had a splinter and was calling for the ski patrol! Meanwhile, it was Saturday, and we were slammed. There were actual injuries all over the mountain, and instead of helping people who were legitimately hurt, I was standing there with this guy who had a splinter.

I looked at his face and realized that he looked familiar. I was trying to place the face as he complained about his splinter, and I realized that he was my girlfriend's ex-boyfriend. We had never met, but I must have recognized him from a picture.

I was a dedicated ski patroller, but this seemed ridiculous.

"Dude," I said, "you gotta take care of your own splinter."

I couldn't wait to get home and tell my girlfriend about her ex-boyfriend's "injury."

Leanne

In addition to showing up, it's also really important to know when it's time to call it and let something go.

My first husband and I entered into our marriage with great love and great intentions and tried our best to make it work. We had dated long-distance for two or three years and didn't live in the same city until right before we were married. That was our fatal flaw: we never had the opportunity to get to know each other on a daily basis, in "real life," if you will.

My first husband is an amazing man with a thousand attributes going for him, and I can see why I fell for him and why we thought we could make it. But there is a natural and unquantifiable connection that two people who are creating a life together should have—and we never had it. We were good on paper, yes, but we never took the time to see if we were good in 3-D before we took our vows.

I put him through a lot of intense conversations that maybe were never actually necessary. I was trying to change a human into something else, but he really didn't need to change; it was our combination that was the problem, not him.

We ended our marriage about four years later with the same love and respect that we started it with. I remember, during the phone conversation that closed the door, beautiful light pouring into the room. He ended the call by saying, "I love you, Leanne. I'll call tomorrow to check on you."

I said, "I love you too." And the next day, just like he said he would, he called to check in.

After my divorce I took a year to be alone. One solid year to myself. I also wanted to be sure that I was happy and healthy and strong on my own. I didn't want to dive into another relationship while still half-broken.

I figured I could sit and wallow in my failure and my sadness of being a divorced woman at thirtysomething—or I could rebrand it. I could flip failure on its head.

I named my single year "the Freedom Tour," and I got busy living. I decided I was going to do new things I couldn't have done if I had stayed on the path I was on. I took trips and read books and went dancing. I drove through the desert and ran around Texas, honky-tonking. I went to Paris with friends, and we drank wine and wrote poetry and went dancing under the Seine River. We wore ball gowns to walk around the streets of Cannes for no other reason than that we were in Cannes! I had a midnight tea party in London with old friends. I stayed true to myself and didn't jump into a serious relationship with anyone prematurely. And I ended up having an amazing year.

The end of a relationship hurts—no doubt about it. But I knew it was time to let go. And looking back, what has stayed and what stands out to me is not the pain of the heartbreak but the power and healing that I experienced when I found a way to redeem the failure.

This holds true not only when relationships end but when we have unexpected road bumps in our careers. In fact, I think everybody should get fired at least once in their lives.

Steve

I don't think I've ever been fired.

Leanne

Good, Steve. I have. Twice. And you know what? Losing those jobs was the best thing that could have happened to my career.

The first time I got fired was at my Betsey Johnson internship between junior and senior year in college, before I worked for Heatherette. I actually had the chance to work with the legend herself that summer. She was a pistol, and a joy and a light to be around. One day she pulled me from whatever it was I was doing and asked me to come try on these incredible vintage pieces because her fit model didn't show up. There I was, standing in the office in the strangest little outfit you ever did see, trying to play it cool and overhearing Betsey talking about how she first showed this look in some basement New York bar with Velvet Underground playing, while she sat next to her friend Andy Warhol. That was a memory for the books.

I got along really well with all my fellow interns. We had an amazing time in and out of the office. And I loved hanging out with the women in the public relations department; because of those interactions I became fascinated by marketing. I loved the energy and excitement and camaraderie those women shared, and watching them work gave me a whole new perspective on the business of design.

Of course there were parts of the job that weren't glamorous, but that's true of any internship. So I bopped around that office like a ray of sunshine. And I wasn't ashamed of it. I'm me, and I can't be anyone else but me.

One day, my boss pulled me in her office and told me to take a seat. I knew it wasn't going to be good. She had a dour look on her face.

"Leanne, we're going to fire you," she said.

"Why are you firing me?" I asked. "I've been working very hard!"

I really had been. I had learned so much there and was having a great experience.

She replied, "You're having *too* much fun."

The words from an old country song came to mind: "I ain't never had too much fun."

"Fire me?" I said. "But I'm working for free!"

That did not change her mind.

"I just got fired from a *free* job," I said to my parents when I called them. I was so confused. "This is so bad."

Except it was perfectly fine. It was *better* than fine. I went back to Ohio University, where I contemplated my new fashion trajectory. *If this is fashion, I need to rethink my career.*

I never actually got into fashion design—I got into fashion *marketing*. Because of that one experience and that one brilliant failure, all of my jobs after that leaned toward marketing. All because I got fired. From a free job. (Sorry, just had to say that part again.)

I also got fired from my one and only corporate job, which was at a surf and skate company in Orange County, California. I had been there for about two or three months when the woman who hired me was replaced. The boss who initially hired me gave me wings and support; I was open to learning from her and *wanted* to learn from her. I wanted to help her succeed. I felt lucky to be in her presence. But my new boss and I never quite clicked, and it wasn't long before I was miserable.

I don't even remember the specific incident that was the straw that broke the camel's back, but eventually I felt I had to speak up.

"I'd like to talk to you. Can we meet tomorrow?" I emailed her.

"Sure. How about 8:00 a.m.?" she wrote back.

I got there at 8:00 a.m. for this meeting that *I* thought *I* had called, and my boss was there with the lawyer to fire me.

Ouch.

That was my one and only year working in the corporate world. *If that's what corporate culture is like,* I thought, *then no thank you.* And this company wasn't your average corporate world; we used to skateboard in the office! I realized, *If this is too corporate for me, there ain't no use going anywhere else.* Working in a traditional office environment was just another idea I needed to let go of.

I have to be honest: I welcomed being fired. Because sometimes you need a push out the door. I was just staying there for the money, and that's not enough.

I don't live to work; I work to live. That's been very important to me my whole career. My first career goal is to have a happy, nice life, and my second career goal is to create. I'm not trying to win something or make it somewhere. Is it for the glory? No. Fame? No. Money? No. I just want to create.

There are so many successful people who got fired and who then succeeded. Marc Jacobs got fired from Perry Ellis before moving on to Louis Vuitton and, eventually, starting his own company.[2] J. K. Rowling got fired because she was too busy brainstorming ideas.[3] Anna Wintour, the editor of *Vogue*, got fired as a junior editor at *Harper's Bazaar*. In 2010, at a *Teen Vogue* conference, she told the audience, "I recommend you all get fired. It's a great learning experience."[4] There are countless examples of people who turned their lives around—if that's even what you could call it.

Here's my point: whether I was at the end of a relationship or the end of a job, I took something that could have been deflating and bad and said, *What good could come from this? How can I make this a happy ending?* Of course, in the moment, it's hard to see the positive. You feel as if the world's ended. But what if you flipped that script and said, *Hmmm . . . Now what? The whole world is open to me. The whole world is ahead of me. I can live anywhere. I can do anything. I can go anywhere.* There's a beautiful freedom to losing the path you thought you were on, really.

Getting fired also taught me how to be a good boss. Because of that experience, I'm always mindful about giving people who work for me their wings—freedom to work on their own. I don't want to micromanage everything.

I actually had this conversation with my team from the television show yesterday: "I want you guys to be able to make decisions and do things without a constant check-in from me." They're a smart group of people. They're here to make the show great. And they're working on it because they want to grow skills. They want to get experience. I'm sure every one of them will work on past me, and I want to encourage that. Moreover, I want to help them do that! If I'm your employer, I don't want you to work for me forever. I want you to go to your *own* company. I want you to do your own thing, and while you're here helping me, how much can we learn together? I'm a mindful boss because of my experiences.

I don't want to be a Pollyanna here (though I do love her). I'm not dismissing the part of failure that hurts or the part of failure that makes you feel down. You have to mourn the loss first. Wallow in that sadness if you need to; sometimes life just deserves a good cry. But don't stop there. Let go of what you've lost, and embrace the freedom that's in front of you.

WORKING ON PROGRESS

What "failure" in your life can you give yourself a break on?

Think of a past failure that really affected you; then, with the benefit of hindsight, make a list of what good came out of that failure.

Think of someone who denied you what you thought you wanted at the time—a job, a relationship, anything—and send out love to that person for sending you on the path you were supposed to be on the whole time.

Next time something in your life doesn't go as planned, yell, "Plot twist" and carry on! (And yes, I stole that from a meme.)

And this is my favorite "trick": say to God, "All yours, God. Take it from here. Your call!" Now relax. It's all taken care of.

5

The Lucky Ones

A good father is one of the most unsung,
unpraised, unnoticed, and yet one of the
most valuable assets in our society.

–BILLY GRAHAM

Leanne

My favorite memory of my dad is his laughter. He was always laughing. My friends and I would be playing in the basement and hear him laughing through the floorboards. *America's Funniest Home Videos* (*AFV*) really got him! It was a Ford family favorite. That and *Three Amigos*, if that tells you anything. I mean, sometimes he would be laughing so hard he would be pounding the floor with his foot. And, no joke, one night my friend Elisabeth and I were trying to "teach school" over the ruckus of *AFV* (she and I were in our make-believe classroom down in the laundry room), and we heard this huge thud. Dad had been laughing so hard that he rolled off the sofa.

That's my memory of our childhood home. So much joy.

Dad's memories of his own childhood always revolved around food. On my honor, the only thing Dad must have done during his childhood was eat. His favorite saying, of many dad joke–type sayings, was, "Donuts for breakfast, hot dogs for lunch, pizza for dinner." As we got older, this was totally not the case; as a family we started eating healthy, but he still claimed the motto. So it's no surprise that some of my best times with Dad revolved around food too. Mainly the big DQ—that's Dairy Queen for you less-traveled types. Usually, we would head to Office Depot (our favorite hangout) and then off to Dairy Queen. What can I say? We liked to party.

We'd cruise through town in Dad's beige (he called it *champagne*) Ford Taurus, crack the moonroof, and blast the *Cocktail* soundtrack. It was pretty much a guarantee that we would have to rewind and repeat "Don't Worry, Be Happy" over and over again. It was the Ford family theme song. (If you've never heard it, stop reading and put it on!)

Life in the Ford family was good. It was *Leave It to Beaver*, *The Brady Bunch*, *Father Knows Best* good. But in a single instant, all of that changed.

In 2004 I was living in New York. I had just finished college. I can remember it so clearly. I had just gotten back to my apartment after having this amazing New York day, and I was making dinner when my phone rang. It was my big sister. To this day I can't imagine how hard it must have been for her to get the words out.

"Dad's gone," she said.

I was twenty-two years old, and my dad had died from a heart attack at age sixty-two.

Steve

It came as a total surprise because he was the healthiest man I'd ever met. He had abs! He went to the gym every day, played tennis all the time. Loved tennis. Tennis is what got him. He was playing tennis with three of his friends, like he always did. They told us afterward how much fun they were all having. How he was laughing right before he fell.

Leanne

I still think about that: how we're all going to experience this kind of loss. *Every one of us.* I remember thinking that *everyone* on the planet will feel this someday in some way. I was at the grocery store, just staring at people, thinking, *Every one of these people will lose, or has already lost, somebody.*

Losing a parent is definitely what you fear most as a child, no matter how old you are. I was in shock. Thank goodness for shock.

I got on the airplane to fly home to Pittsburgh. I was with a friend. "You do not seem like a girl without a dad," he said. I'll always remember him saying that, because I still don't feel like a girl without a dad. Dad was such a strong force. Even now—he's all over this book! My dad's presence in my first twenty-two years on the planet is why I am who I am. I was always loved by my parents, and I always felt seen and heard by them.

Steve

The day Dad died, someone—I don't remember who—called me and said, "Come to the hospital." But I knew right away something was wrong. That day was a turning point and something that came as a complete shock. Losing Dad was the first real tragedy, real hurt and suffering, that any of us, including our mom, had ever experienced.

Leanne

We always talked about how we hoped our parents would die together. Sounds morbid, but that's how much we saw and respected their love for one another.

Our parents had a great love story. They met at Duquesne University. Mom was an undergrad, and Dad was a law student there. Dad saw Mom through a crowd and said, "Who's that girl?"

Mom saw our dad through the crowd and said, "Who's that old guy?"

Dad was so taken by our mom that he planned a mixer between her sorority and his law fraternity just so he could meet her. She walked in and saw him surrounded by giggling, laughing women, all flirting with him. He immediately walked away from that group to talk to her.

"Hi, Jackie," he said.

"Hi," she said, shyly, not knowing how he knew her name. Turns out he had done his research. They hit it off immediately, made each other laugh.

"What's your name?" she asked.

"Snidely Whiplash," he said.

Snidely Whiplash is the villain from *The Rocky and Bullwinkle Show*. He was the diabolical archenemy of Dudley Do-Right. And really, it was just a funny name.

It stayed a joke of Dad's; when they were older and far into their marriage, Mom said they'd go to a café and he'd put his name as Snidely on the wait list.

Dad had a massive funeral. A standing-room-only kind of funeral, which was sweet. He had a lot of friends. We didn't realize how many lives our dad affected until then. People came out of the woodwork. We heard so many stories about how our dad had taken care of so many people, and we just had no idea.

I wish I could have known him now, as an adult, because there are so many things that I want to ask him, so much I want to talk to him about. There are so many books and historical movies and shows that I want to tell him about. And even more, I want to hear what he knows. I wish I had known to ask more questions while I could. We'd be friends. In fact, we were just *starting* to be friends.

I'd been a tough teen to my dad—stubborn mainly. I was always a good kid, but let's just say I got my stubbornness from my dad, and that didn't always make for smooth sailing. I feel bad about that—I wish I'd had more years of friendship with him. But I had some; I had started to grow up. I was just starting to get to know him as a good man instead of as just my dad. I'm so thankful for that.

I find myself acting just like him. I tell bad dad jokes now, the type of jokes I used to roll my eyes at when he would say them. I say them now.

My dad always laughed at his own jokes. I do that now.

Ain't that the way?

So many people have experienced the death of a parent at a young age; we are not the only ones. In fact, we were "lucky" enough to be adults in our twenties when we lost him. But we are still sadly a part of this secret society of kids who have lost a parent, and there are a lot of us. When you experience it, you're more able to relate to others who have gone through it. When you haven't lost anyone, you can be empathetic, but you often don't know what to say, and you never know how they feel. Now when somebody says to me, "You know, my mom died," or

"My dad died," instead of buckling up, I'm thankful that I'm able to say, "I am so sorry. How are you holding up?" and really understand their answer.

All this being said, I feel like I had more of a dad in twenty-two years than most people get in a lifetime. He packed it in! And I have to say, somehow, even through the horrible experience of losing him, I feel *lucky*.

That's right—because he was so present in our formative years. He is why we are who we are.

And how lucky to have someone so amazing to miss. Someone that even my friends miss. Our friends, our extended family, our cousins— seems everybody he interacted with felt more loved by knowing him. A lot of people really took his passing personally because he was *everyone's* dad. Everyone still talks about him. He's definitely not forgotten. My husband never had a chance to meet him, but he says he feels like he knows him so well because of how often we speak about him and because of the love he left behind for us. It's amazing what time does, though. That you're able to smile and function and laugh again. The human spirit is resilient.

Sometimes people lose someone and they don't talk about it anymore, which is a disservice to that person. Talk about the people you miss; talk about the happy memories; talk about how much they would have loved this day, how much you wish they were here. Remember that having had someone in your life that you loved so much is a true joy, no matter how or when it ends.

Though this is a hard thing to write about, I think it's a conversation that people should not be afraid to have. Death is not an embarrassment. People are nervous to talk about death and talk about when they lose someone. They don't want to burden others with their feelings. But I say, get *all* up in those feelings.

You become very aware of your mortality when someone close to you dies. Being so close to your mortality has its good and bad side. I'm the most optimistic pessimist you'll ever meet. The life motto that I seem to have made up somewhere along the way is a little messed up: *The only thing worse than dyin' is livin'.*

I know, I know. But when you look at it from an eternal and hopeful perspective, it's actually kind of beautiful. This life is the hard part. It gets better from here.

I stopped going to church for a while after Dad died. Not out of vengeance or anger, but because it was too close to home. Months and months later, I went to the Times Square Church, which has the most incredible gospel choir. They were celebrating and clapping and dancing and singing a song about the presence of the Lord. And I thought, *Wow. This is exactly what my dad is doing in heaven right now. He's pretty much partying.* I had never felt closer to him. It was a very surreal and awesome experience.

According to the Bible, there's lots of singing and dancing in heaven. Sometimes I like to think that maybe Dad and Johnny Cash are sitting around a bonfire together right now, just singing away. They're probably eating ice cream cones. And they are definitely laughing.

6

Find the Light

*There are better things ahead
than any we leave behind.*

−C. S. LEWIS

Leanne

The word *inspired* comes from the phrase "in spirit." Ask any true creative and they will tell you. Creativity doesn't come *from* you; it comes *through* you. I can take no credit for what I've created, what I've accomplished to this point. I was given the gift—by all truth of the definition—of thinking differently. I have been blessed (or cursed, depending on the day) with a creative mind.

And the gusto to use that creativity? Given to me.

The business savvy to know what to do with it all? Given to me.

Our job as creative souls is to set free our creativity so that it flows from us to the world. Whatever you create—whatever it is—is *meant to be here* on the planet. Don't get in its way.

I can't truly talk about my life, or my path, or my family, or my career without talking about my faith—about my relationship with God. It's in everything I do and don't do, say and don't say. It's why I feel the peace and confidence that I feel and why I have the gusto to go for just about anything. When you think of life in the big picture—and I mean the *big picture*—the little failures, the mess-ups, the comments, and the regrets just don't hold quite as much weight. Actually, they really don't hold any weight.

People always seem to be surprised to find out that I'm a Christian. I'm not sure why; maybe it's because I'm, well, fun! Though I have to say for the record, there are a lot of fun Christians out there. Watch out—we're everywhere! But actually, I think it's probably because they don't really understand what being a Christian is all about. It's not boring, rigid, or narrow-minded. I don't think Jesus was that way either. I have the joy of living a life of love, because I walk around knowing I'm so very loved by God.

Steve

When people ask me about religion, I tend to clam up. In fact, writing about religion is a bit of a strange experience. This is the first time I'm speaking about my commitment to my faith in such a public way, so bear with me.

My close friends all know that I'm a Christian. Most people don't know this about me because I don't usually bring it up, for no other reason except I generally keep things to myself. I'm sort of a private guy that way. I usually go to church by myself on Sundays. Every once in a while, if they want to come, maybe a friend comes.

I kind of keep religion and politics to myself because those conversations can be personal. People are entitled to feel however they want. We can be friends and not entirely agree. I'm certainly not trying to change anybody with my beliefs, but I'm happy to discuss my beliefs if someone asks. I'm certainly not going to judge you if you don't believe what I believe.

What I do want to say is that Young Life (a Christian ministry geared toward students) was one of the most positive influences in my life. I went to many Christian camps growing up, but Young Life camp was always a highlight of my high school years. I appreciated how God was presented in such a fun and positive way. No judgment—just love and meeting kids where they were. For me, Young Life represented acceptance and friendship, and it was a place where I could be me. And I appreciated the adult leaders in Young Life, like Chris Buda, who took an interest in us as we were growing in our faith.

Leanne

We were raised in a Christian household—church every Sunday. It was a big part of our life. When you're a kid, you do whatever your parents do. I went to church with my parents because that's what I was supposed to do. I had a connection through it from my family.

Dad came home for dinner every night, and every night we prayed together as a family. Every Wednesday night for ten years, my family and I went to a youth program at our church. Mom and Dad were both leaders. Dad was the leader of Steve's group, the Royal Rangers. Mom was a leader for the girls' group, the Missionettes. (That would make a great band name, by the way.) Mom even used to say a prayer with us every day before we got on the bus. It was a big part of our family fabric—a part of our family we appreciated.

But then in high school, something shifted in me: my faith became my own.

I was at Young Life. (Michelle, Steve, and I all went to Young Life.) I was taking a walk in the woods at night by myself. This might sound odd—taking a walk in the woods by yourself—but if you have ever been to camp, you know that walking in the woods and having some alone time to think is part of the experience. I remember it clearly. I was looking at the stars. It was a spiritual moment. I understood God's beautiful and full love for me. I trusted him with my life. It was a very aware, adult decision that I came to: that my faith is my own and that Jesus is actually the coolest dude—okay, *God*—to walk the planet. And I was on his team now.

I realized in that moment that I had this connection to God—a spiritual connection. Not because of my parents, not because of my upbringing, but because I chose to for me.

It was a big deal. And the amazing side product of that decision is that it has provided such a safety and emotional freedom for me in every aspect of my life.

Steve

I'm in the woods all the time; maybe that's why I always feel it. Seriously! Spending time in nature is one of the most spiritual things you can do.

I also believe that a lot of the blessings we had as children and adults is because of our faith. I think a lot of good things came from our upbringing. I don't know if it's because of our accountability to our heavenly Father, but I always felt that there was something bigger than me that put me here. It's actually difficult for me to put into words. It's faith—just a gut feeling.

Leanne

My friends always ask why I have such a calm in my life. And I truly believe that it's because my worth comes from more than just what's happening to us and around us here on the earth.

Life is bigger than just who we are. We are not bodies with souls—we are souls with bodies. How wild is that? This is a temporary home for us and a temporary body. There's so much more to life than what our eyes can see. And knowing that, I want to live a life of meaning and purpose. And live it *on* purpose.

The Bible is about a massive amount of love. That's how I want to live my life.

I would like to think of myself as a nonjudgmental Christian. Unfortunately, there have been a lot of Christians who think it's their job to be the morality police and go around telling everyone that they're wrong. Well, we all have different beliefs—and I follow Jesus—but God has called me to love others regardless of our differences. Far too often, we have lost the joy of Christianity in the translation. Jesus came with a message of joy and love and hope—all good things! He didn't come to judge us; he came to *love* us. Of course, humans tend to mess up everything, so we judge each other and say it's in the name of God. That's the *opposite* of the message in the Bible. The Bible is a very long love letter to us. Jesus came to bring peace and love and hope, and he laid down his life to do so. That's why it's called "good news"!

Even before I had this spiritual awakening at camp, I felt a confidence because of my faith.

I didn't feel peer pressure in high school. Honestly, I couldn't have cared less if people thought I was cool or not cool. I'd go to the parties in high school, and I'd dance and have fun, but every once in a while, someone would always get mad at me because I wasn't drinking. If I'm not judging you and mad at you that you *are* drinking, why are you mad at me for not drinking?

It's one of the biggest things I want to instill in my kiddo: I want her to feel strongly about what she believes and not worry about what others think about it.

I didn't need to impress anyone as a teenager. This was good, because I don't think I had much to offer to be impressive anyway at that point in life. But I had a real sense of self. I didn't need friends to tell me I was cool. If you don't need to find your worth from the world, it really gives you a sense of peace in life. It's called "the peace that passes understanding" (Philippians 4:7, paraphrased). It takes the stress off of what other people are thinking and saying and allows you to live your life with joy and a sense of serenity.

Steve

Well, I've already shared quite a bit about how little I cared about what people thought of me back in high school. But I will say that my faith was a real comfort when Dad died. I'm looking forward to seeing him and being together again.

7

No Guts, No Story

Live, travel, adventure, bless, and don't be sorry.
—JACK KEROUAC

Leanne

I haven't quite figured out if being driven is a blessing or a curse. Both, I guess. When you always have the urge to go-go-go, in every sense of the word, I can only guess there's a reason for it, this unrest. It kind of makes you wonder, what is God pushing you toward? What adventures are ahead of you that you don't even know to wish for yet?

At twenty-three I had been in New York City for a while, and city living was getting to me. It was tough being so poor in New York, and I was longing for warmer weather. I used to walk past the Roxy store in Times Square and watch the huge screen above with videos of these girls laughing and surfing. I'd dream of the sun shining down on my face. I always had an attachment to Quiksilver and Roxy. I know I'm just a Pittsburgh girl, but I have always loved surf and skate culture. I'd look at their gorgeous window displays decorated with sunny, happy faces. I started dreaming of beaches and the Pacific Ocean, warm weather and sunny days. I wanted to be where they were.

Instead, it was raining, and I was in the subway, with drenched bell bottoms. They were like little mops soaking up the Times Square puddles, the water up to the knees of my jeans at this point. (Note to self: don't wear bell bottoms in the rain.)

On the subway that day, there was a cute girl and a cute guy sitting across from me. They were just being silly and having fun. They were drenched, but they weren't miserable like I was.

"You're not from around here, are you?" I said to these total strangers.

"How'd you know?" they said.

"Because you're having too much fun," I said, smiling.

Of course, I had plenty of fun times in New York, but that day, I was a mess. I had hit a low.

"Do you work for Roxy?" I asked the girl.

She had a major tip-off: she was wearing head-to-toe Roxy logos.

"Yes, I do! How'd you know?" she asked.

Lucky guess.

We immediately hit it off, and we decided to get drinks. Turns out that she was the head of marketing for Roxy—*the* California brand that I had been dreaming of. And she asked if I wanted to come for an interview.

Yes, for real. Even as I write this, I am thinking, *Man, we should all talk to more strangers!*

For the interview they flew me to Los Angeles—*they* flew *me*. (It was a big deal!) It was an absolute whirlwind. I was standing on the hotel balcony, staring out at the ocean from my hotel room, on the phone with Mom. "I have a hotel room in Huntington Beach! And they are paying for it!"

Soon after, I was hired to work with the public relations team at Roxy. Aaah!

Every season, when a new line of clothing drops, a fashion brand like Roxy sends samples of their collection to magazines; the editors use these pieces in their editorial shoots or for lay downs in the pages of their magazine. My job in the PR department was to send these samples. This meant I was in charge of the sample closet.

Let's just say the sample closet needed some love. It needed to be cleaned, organized, and—most important—edited. So I did a major edit, picking out the most interesting pieces and ditching clothes that weren't as special. I sent editors only the best pieces from that season. I would curate and choose what they saw based on which magazine was asking, as well as what the photoshoot story was about. I worked with *Vogue* and *Elle* and *People*. Editors started to notice. I heard people talking about it; they were saying, "Roxy's getting so good."

It's all about the edit. I was being very calculated about the style of the magazine and what they needed and what the story needed. I was curating Roxy carefully for each of them. I was also gifting Roxy pieces to celebrities. You can imagine my twenty-three-year-old reaction when I came into work one morning to a voice mail from Sarah Jessica Parker, thanking me for her gift. That was a pass-the-phone-around-for-everyone-to-hear kind of message!

Dana Dartez was the head of design at Roxy at the time, and she started to notice what I was doing with the clothes, as well as how I personally was wearing them. She took me under her wing. She loved me and, it turned out, more important for my career, she loved my style.

She asked me to come help her on a photo shoot. This was not normal, to pull someone out from the PR team to help with the styling, by the way. I was thrilled. I mean, *thrilled*. A real live photo shoot! It was the first professional shoot I had ever been on. She knew it too. She coached me on what to do and not do and showed me what she needed help with. She gave me racks and racks of the clothes from the new season and told me to put together outfits I would wear.

I jumped in. I assisted her however she needed on that shoot, helping put looks together, dressing the models, and adding details that made the outfits and images more special. I brought a bunch of old shell necklaces and ropes and vintage pieces to add some oomph.

We talked through and tweaked how the clothes fit, how the models sat, where they sat. We added Mexican blankets and fun props, anything we needed to make the shoot special. I'm telling you *that very day* and *that very shoot* resparked my love of fashion. More important, it started my love of photo shoots and launched my styling career. Dana is the reason I got into styling; it changed the trajectory of my career and my life. Thank you, Dana!

Looking back, I never missed an opportunity that was put in front of me. I would say yes to everything. Ever heard the phrase "Fake it till you make it"? That's my life. Jump in and learn as you go. If you have *it*, you will know! Some things can't be learned; some things just have to naturally flow out of your brain. That's the "it" factor.

I'm thankful to Dana for picking me out of a building of people and asking me to help on her shoot. Mentors are crucial in any business. I always think about that and always want to do the same for the people who are talented newbies helping me now. How can we encourage people to grow, to try things? How can we give them opportunities they wouldn't have otherwise? It is our job to inspire, encourage, teach, and push each other forward.

Steve

You had moved to California, and I was dreaming of moving there too. I was finishing a job in Pittsburgh, selling home remodeling. I was selling roofing, windows, siding, and doors. I wasn't crazy about being a salesman in that field—would have rather been an installer, probably. But I tried a different career path, and I wasn't feeling it.

The good news was that I was able to pay off all my debt, clear up my credit cards, and save some money. I decided it was time for a change. So I wrote the date February 16 on my mirror. It would be my target date to leave Pittsburgh and drive to California. If I wrote it down on my mirror, that's when I knew I would make it happen. My goal was to have everything situated and ready—have enough money, have a plan. A mirror is a good place to write a goal. Why? Because you look at your mirror (almost) every day.

Leanne

But does he?

Steve

My goal was pretty simple: I wanted to be a surfer. That was it. I fig-ured I'd pick up odd jobs and concentrate on the ocean. After all, I was only twenty-six years old, so this wasn't a difficult plan. I had no responsibilities, all my debts were paid, I had a car, all my money was in the bank, and I thought, *Why not?* So I asked Leanne if I could crash on her couch for a while.

I drove across country in a Toyota truck. It was my dream truck as a child after seeing *Back to the Future*. My dream car wasn't the DeLorean; it was the truck that Marty McFly drove. When I got my job as a salesman, I was able to buy myself that truck. See, I can be very practical when I want to be!

It only took me two days to drive across country. I just made a beeline to California. Leanne had a roommate, Shilpa, and was living in Long Beach. She probably expected me to stay for a little while until I found a place of my own. But that wasn't my goal. My goal was to be a professional freeloader.

I know that sounds a little crazy, but if you had your younger sister living in California, wouldn't you do the same? I wanted to go full surfer mode. No timeline, no strings attached, no expectations or goals.

And I thought I was a pretty good guest. I found an empty cabinet in her kitchen and put all my clothes in the cabinet and hid all my stuff in her house so it didn't look like I was sleeping on the couch or staying there for a long period of time. I was gone most of the time. Really! They probably only saw me when they woke up in the middle of the night or in the morning. I was trying to be a considerate freeloader.

Eventually, they both let me know that I should be paying rent. The nerve!

My freeloading didn't last very long. I got the vibe from Leanne and her roommate that this wasn't exactly how they imagined living: in a nice apartment in Long Beach with Leanne's older brother sleeping on the couch. Eventually, I moved in with a friend of mine who lived in Santa Monica. But soon, he and I got an apartment in Studio City, which is very far from the beach. Technically, it's not that far, but with the traffic, it sometimes took me an hour to get to the beach. I was thinking, *Why am I even in California?* Suddenly, my full-time surfing dreams were put on hold.

Looking back, it was not the most well-hatched plan. It was probably meant to be temporary—how long can you live on someone's couch and surf? I think I pushed it to its limit and had fun doing it.

Thanks, Leanne!

Leanne

Okay. Let's talk about this, Steve. I'm pretty sure you just invented the phrase *considerate freeloader.* Couple of things to note here:

1. Steve totally tricked us. He just kept staying there and staying there. We didn't know that he had moved in to our place. He failed to mention that.

2. Steve is six foot five—he thinks he was sneaking around and we didn't even "notice" that he was there? He wasn't exactly invisible in our tiny little apartment, thank you very much.

3. I remember when we told Steve if he was planning on staying, then he had to start chipping in. He was shocked—like, *offended* that I asked.

4. I'd like to put out a formal apology to my roommate, Shilpa, for putting up with me and my big—in every sense of the word— brother as long as she did. Shilpa, thank you, and I'm sooooooo sorry.

As my career carried on, I started to build relationships with magazine editors. I had been at Roxy for about a year when Monika Steinberg, the editor-in-chief of *Foam*, a women's surf magazine, asked me to be their fashion editor.

"Uh, yup!" I said.

This was a new world for me, one I wouldn't have even thought to aspire to. She wanted me to create, produce, direct, style, and run three shoots an issue, using all the different surf brand collections. She believed I was up for the task.

I had never been a fashion editor, of course, which meant I had no true experience with running a photo shoot, let alone had a portfolio. It was a crucial time, a moment that could change my entire career. But I needed help. So I called a friend, Erik Lang, a photographer I met at David LaChapelle's office while I was working for Heatherette. Erik was the studio manager there, but was also a great (and more important, young and hungry) photographer.

"I'm doing a magazine shoot for *Foam*," I said to Erik. "I have no idea what I am doing. Want to shoot it?"

As you may have noticed, I have no shame. I completely believe in asking people for help when you need it. You have to put yourself out there or you will not move forward in life. The worst that can happen is that someone will say no. Good people inherently want to help each other. Erik was on board.

With that said, I didn't know what I was doing, and the shoot was, dare I say, subpar. I chose way too many locations. I was overzealous, if you will. It was freezing, we were shooting swim, and we were having the models change their clothes in the car. It was pretty much torture. Everything was wrong. But I guess I didn't know much better. I felt so bad for that crew. They were troopers!

I brought my work back to Monika at *Foam*. Remember: this was my interview for the job as fashion editor. But it was all I had. I sat nervously in her office.

"What did you learn about this shoot?" Monika asked me.

"I learned to get a trailer with heat for the models," I said.

Let's just say she agreed. Yet she hired me, bless her soul. She knew I had the ability to take on the job, even though I didn't have any formal training or experience. But I had moxie, and I had style, and I had the drive to figure it out.

I was the fashion editor at *Foam* for a few years. I did all parts of every shoot: creative direction, production, and styling. Finding new creative ways to show the same style of clothes over and over. I loved it! I worked with some amazing talents, models, photographers, hair and makeup stylists—people I still admire to this day.

Whatever you dream of doing—do it. Do it for free; do it for fun; do it for the love of it. People will be drawn to your gusto, to your spirit, and, therefore, to your craft. And if you're lucky—and you will be one day—someone is going to pay you to do what you would otherwise do for free. As the saying goes: "Fortune favors the brave." I still can't believe people pay me to create!

Steve

While Leanne was working at Roxy and *Foam*, I was making my way up the ranks as a background actor. Yes, I'm serious. Basically, it's a great way to make a little money if you live in Los Angeles. I went through a central casting company. All you had to do was show up, and you'd work on the movie set all day, and they'd feed you—just for standing there in the background of their shows or movies.

I also worked some construction while I was out there. There was a house being built down the street from Leanne's place, and I walked over there one day with my hammer and my tool belt.

"Are you hiring?" I said. "Because I need a job."

I did some framing at that house, and that turned into a few other jobs. Ultimately, the stories from Central Casting were more fun and exciting than the ones from my construction jobs—even though I was learning a lot on the construction jobs.

It's amazing how many shows you can do as a background actor. I did a number of TV shows, like *Jericho, House, Numb3rs,* and *The Office.* I also did a couple of movies, like *Live Free or Die Hard* and *Dreamgirls.*

Dreamgirls was my real claim to fame as a background actor because I was actually in the movie for about two whole seconds.

In 2006, *Dreamgirls* was playing on Christmas Day in theaters across the country. Leanne and I went home to Pittsburgh for Christmas, and we went with my entire family to see the movie together because I was in it. Let me tell you: it was the longest movie ever. It was especially long when your family is sitting there just to see you. I'm just in the background, and my big "role" doesn't come on until the end. The camera starts on my face and then pans away. I got a solid two seconds of major motion picture time.

Leanne

Watching Steve in *Dreamgirls*—or should I say *waiting* to watch Steve in *Dreamgirls*—was amazing. He took the entire family with him over Christmas holiday to see his big film debut.

We waited.

And we waited.

And they started singing another song, and we waited. No Steve.

Finally, he told us *this* was his scene. He was thrilled. Here he comes—and nothing. His scene was him and about a thousand other extras in a crowd. We kind of shrugged and looked at each other.

"Great job, Steve. Sorry we couldn't see you." We were pretty disappointed.

All of a sudden, Steve's face comes up on the entire screen. And only his face—in a Fu Manchu–style mustache, mind you. We all screamed and jumped up and down. The entire family was high-fiving and hugging there in the theater. And that was that; the movie went on for some more musical numbers like nothing ever happened.

I laugh every time I think about that day. We have to watch it again, Steve!

Speaking of stars of the family, and not to outdo Steve's Hollywood debut, but this was around the time the real star of our family showed up, Tom Ford the dog. Yes, that's really his name.

I adopted Tom while I was living in LA, shortly after my dad died. He's about seventeen years old now. And he's still going strong, thank you very much. His full adopted name was "Turbo Tripod Tom," Tom for short. And of course he took my last name, so there ya go. Tom is a true gentleman, the self-proclaimed president of the Scrappy Dogs club, with his big, droopy eyes and rock 'n' roll haircut. He's invincible.

While I was living in Long Beach, there was an article in the local magazine that read "Save These Dogs." All the dogs had full body pictures, but not little Tom; he only had a side profile of his face. *This dog got dissed*, I thought.

We grew up with West Highland terriers, and I loved terrier faces. So I kept talking about Tom, how cute Tom was. I wanted to meet him.

Finally, my friend threw me his phone. "Call Tom," he said.

I called and asked, "Is Tom there?"

The owners were so excited that I called. The woman on the other end, his foster mom, started telling me all about Tom.

"He's a little pistol. A charmer with the ladies," she said. She was going on and on about Tom this and Tom that. Then, after about forty-five minutes, she said, "So we cut it off."

"Wait a minute," I said. "Cut what off?"

Apparently, Tom had come to them with a broken leg. They couldn't fix it, so they had to amputate it. Tom is a three-legged dog.

"I'll be right over," I said.

Tom was a little gray scruffy guy, maybe about ten pounds soaking wet. He's got one back leg, so he hobbles around.

I had found the dog of my dreams, a perfectly imperfect pup who needed a home.

"He's perfect," I said.

"Well, if you think he's perfect, you better take him," the lady said. "Because no one else wants him."

But I wanted him. I wanted him *because* of what he looked like. This is what Tom has always looked like, for all of his seventeen years. He's always looked like an old man and a puppy dog at the same time.

When Tom goes to the bathroom, he does a full-on handstand. Yes, a handstand. He lifts his back leg and stands on his two front legs. It's his best party trick; it's very impressive!

Tom's a little nomad scrapper. He has lived with me in Long Beach, in Pittsburgh, in Nashville, in LA, and in New York. He's driven across country four times with me. Tom may not be a looker, but he's absolutely perfect for me. When I say "I love you, Tom," he stops whatever he's doing to come over and give me a little doggy kiss. Then he goes right back to what he was up to, which—let's face it—is usually snoozing or eating. He's added such joy to my life. He's lying beside me right now, probably reading over my shoulder.

———————

While Steve, Tom, and I had a great time in California, you've probably noticed that I'm a bit of a wanderer. I actually love every phase of what

I'm doing, but then, I tend to move on. I love new adventures. I love traveling.

I remember watching a documentary about Vincent Van Gogh when I was maybe twenty. I was fascinated by the fact that he didn't even know he could paint before he was twenty-six[1]—he had never picked up a paintbrush! It got me thinking, *What if there's something I am good at that I didn't even know I could do?* I decided that twenty-six was going to be my "Van Gogh year," and maybe I, too, would find something I was good at that I didn't even know I had skill for.

Then I forgot about it. On my twenty-eighth birthday I remembered my idea of the Van Gogh year and thought, *Oh, shoot. I missed it.* Then I realized, *Wait a second. No, I didn't.*

This is the story of my Van Gogh year.

I decided on a whim to pack up all my stuff in California and move to Nashville. It had enough of a creative industry that I could continue to style and do photo shoots. And I have always loved the South. Plus, in Nashville, I could afford to rent a house and have a yard for Tom. So I decided I was going to give it a try. I packed little Tom Ford and all my worldly belongings into my old Toyota Land Cruiser and hit the highway.

"What are you going to do in Nashville?" someone said to me. "Go be a hick?"

Uh, not exactly.

I was drawn to Nashville for so many reasons. Music is my favorite art form. I love classic country music. No one in my life—meaning folks in my New York and Los Angeles worlds—understood what country music was about. Once, I had to go to a Willie Nelson concert *by myself* because none of my friends knew who Willie Nelson was. Blasphemy. I realized, *If my friends don't like Willie Nelson, I'm in the wrong town!*

In Nashville, I rented a house—an actual three-bedroom house!—for the first time in my life. I found two roommates to share the space and the rent. In the end, I was paying $200 a month. In New York, my room alone cost four times that.

The question of what I would I do for a living wasn't a problem. I was already a stylist, coming from the big city, and I had a large portfolio to prove it. I had a very exciting wow moment: *I'll just go style the country singers.*

Taking risks is part of my M.O.: With Mom's kitchen cabinets. With her refrigerator. With Heatherette. With Roxy. With the way I got into fashion. And now with jumping into the big leagues with some of the best and most well-known musicians in the world.

Steve

Every day Leanne and I take risks. Lately, we've been taking so many risks with people's homes that I would love to take *fewer* risks—or maybe that's just how I'm feeling right now. Working on this show is one of the most challenging jobs I've been part of.

I'm not afraid of taking chances for myself either. Because if you want something bad enough, you don't really worry about the risks. You just think, *I'm going to make it happen.*

Okay, let me reword that: if there is something I want so deeply, then it doesn't feel like a risk. It feels like the *right thing*, rather than a risk.

Leanne

Totally. That's how I felt about Nashville. It felt like the right thing.

I got to Nashville and connected with a small fashion agency there right away; they started sending me on some amazing jobs. I styled

Miranda Lambert for a magazine, Jason Aldean's album cover, Lee Ann Womack for award shows and *Good Morning America*. In fact, Diane Sawyer told Lee Ann Womack that she loved her shoes on national TV—the shoes I chose for her! Fun!

I worked with and met some really fun people. I lived in Nashville for three years and had some incredible experiences there.

It was also the place where I officially became a songwriter. Bet you didn't see that one coming!

Sometimes, words come out of me rhyming. The poem comes out of me without me doing anything. In fact, I've never actually been able to write a poem when I have tried. It would just roll out, and I would write it down however it was, wherever I was, on the back of a check or in the margins of a book. Now I use my phone, thankfully. But before, I used to grab a napkin.

I had tons and tons of writing, piles of it. And I never did a thing with any of it, until I moved to Tennessee.

When I moved to Nashville, my friends were all musicians—some well-known and some not so well-known. We were all poor and happy running around town together. Any time any friends would be at a loss for words and need lyrics, I would dig into my box of poems and find something that matched the mood they were in. That's when my friends started turning my poems into songs.

Hearing someone sing my poetry is one of the greatest thrills I've felt in my career, and it still is pretty much my favorite creative outlet ever. It's so fun.

My friend Nikki Lane turned a poem of mine, called "If You Take Him," into a song. It was the first time I'd heard my words sung. It was something I'd written to Dolly Parton's "Jolene" character. Nikki sang it and emailed it to me one day. I was hooked. (I still think she should put it on her album someday!)

91

Then there was my new friend Jess Maros. She was an amazing singer and guitar player and she wanted to write, but she didn't have a ton of lyrics. We'd met at a clothing party I hosted. My clothing parties are pretty much just that: I swapped and sold clothes to my friends. I made a lot of great girlfriends that way—and paid my rent.

Anyway, Jess came over, and we wrote this song from one of my poems called "Rodeo Queen." It's a song about a girl waiting for her rodeo man to come home from his travels. We had the best time writing this song, and pretty soon after we wrote it, we played it for my friend Tyler James.

Tyler started putting this beat to the song. We were just sitting there in his family room, and all of a sudden, this song turned into a *living, breathing, amazing* song. That day the two of them started their band Escondido, a dreamy, country desert rock band. Several of the songs on that first album, *The Ghost of Escondido*, were written with my poems.

They just put their third album out, and I have a couple of songs on there. In fact, there's a song called "Cold October" that is all about my first big breakup. Escondido performed the song on *Conan O'Brien!* I was backstage on *Conan*, watching my best friends playing a song that I helped write. It was so awesome, and I was so proud of them. Talk about tears! The excitement was like nothing I could compare it to.

We've had songs in movies and on television. A big TV show asked for another one of our songs just recently. So I get what they call "mailbox money." I get a small check every month. It's my biggest thrill. And here's a fun fact: Escondido and I actually wrote the theme song that you hear at the beginning of *Restored By the Fords*. It's called "Roam On Home." You can hear the entire song on their album *Warning Bells*. These things don't happen on their own. I wanted to write these songs with my friends, so I put that out there to them— and they took it.

Here I was, writing songs in Nashville and taking on styling jobs, but I was also living a kind of poor artist's life. And I was always looking for ways to make extra money. One day, I was at a gas station in Nashville and found this dusty old box of vintage sunglasses, mostly from the '80s. They were selling them for fifty cents each. They were just dead stock, collecting dust. The gas station didn't know what to do with them. So I bought a bunch, and I started selling them to my friends for ten dollars. I had a huge box of them, and I never told anybody where I got them. When I ran out, I'd go to the gas station and buy a hundred more.

One year, Nikki and I wanted to go to South by Southwest (SXSW), the massive music, film, and media festival in Austin, but we had no money for gas. We were both so broke.

"I have an idea," I said. We went to the gas station and bought all the sunglasses.

The guy at the gas station looked at me funny.

"What do you want with all these?"

I didn't want him to know that I was making a profit off of them. So I fibbed.

"I'm having sunglasses parties!" I said.

Nikki and I had hundreds of pairs of sunglasses. We loaded up the car and drove to Austin that day, drove thirteen hours. We set up a blanket and a vintage mirror outside one of the bars at SXSW, and we started hocking the shades out of an old suitcase. We were these two cute little hippie girls, yelling, "Shady business! Shady business, here! The future is bright. Gotta wear shades!"

We called our new little endeavor "Gas Money Glasses," and we were the "Shady Ladies." We made thousands of dollars! I kid you not—*thousands* of dollars. We carried a suitcase from spot to spot, and we'd just sit down and open our suitcase. We got some press out of it.

We were in *WGSN*, a trend forecasting company publication. We even had a few celebrity clients.

We were never a legit business. We paid for our gas and then split a big old pile of cash. We kept going back to SXSW, and we had repeat customers. People would see us and say, "There's the Shady Ladies!"

After two years selling those gas station glasses, we ran out of stock. Hey, it was fun while it lasted, and we got our gas money. Success!

Steve

While Leanne was out there in Nashville, selling Gas Money Glasses and writing songs, I decided to go back to Pittsburgh and open a clothing store. Which, of course, sold Gas Money Glasses.

Yes, that's right. I, Steve Ford, the guy who wears the same black T-shirt every day, had a clothing store.

How did it happen that I decided to open a clothing store? Well, when I lived in California, I was working with a guy named Steve Coe, whom I actually met through Leanne.

Leanne

When I met Steve Coe, I knew immediately you would hit it off. "You should be friends with my brother," I told him. And then you were.

Imagine two of Steve. That's what it's like when Steve Ford and Steve Coe are together. Both big beer-drinking, big-dreaming, burly men, only one of them has a British accent. Actually, that's a perfect description: Steve Coe is Steve Ford with a British accent.

Steve

Steve Coe owned a brand called Worn Free. He sold rock 'n' roll T-shirts. He would take John Lennon's "Working Class Hero" slogan, license the image, and then put it on a T-shirt. I worked with Steve on and off for two years. Yes, that's around the time I was freeloading off Leanne and her roommate—well, while I wasn't surfing or framing houses.

It was a great time in my life because I was surfing almost every day, but after a while, it became a little too unstable. I couldn't just keep doing work for Steve Coe, framing houses part-time, and surfing. My surfing-every-day plan kind of washed away (pun intended), and I felt like my life needed more purpose—a bigger commitment.

"I don't know what I'm doing with myself," I said to Steve Coe. "I think I need to move back home and figure out my next career move."

"You're always talking about opening up a store," he said. "Why don't you open a store?"

"How am I going to do that? I'm broke," I said.

And I *was* broke. But I had been hanging out with all these guys who were artists and who were starting T-shirt brands. They were creative people. If they asked me for help, I would say yes. I helped them with construction work and whatever else they needed. That's the kind of guy I am.

"Talk to your friends who are starting T-shirt brands," Steve Coe said. "I'm sure they'll give you clothes to sell."

This is something Leanne spoke about too—you have to be able to ask people for help.

I met up with this group of guys who were all creating interesting artwork. There was Buff Monster, the graffiti artist. There was Steve Aoki, the musician, record producer, and DJ, who was running his record label and lifestyle brand, Dim Mak. I was also friends with another artist who just went by the name Rama. I loved hanging out with these guys because they were so inspirational. They were carving their own paths for themselves.

I always tried to work with them and offer my work to them. At the time, I was trying to figure out my life, so it was really influential and inspirational to work around artists.

One day, I was talking to Rama and he told me he had a back stock of sweaters and hats and sweatshirts they had been making.

"Here. Take all this stuff, and you can sell it by consignment," he said.

Once I spoke to my friends, it was like magic: I drove back to Pittsburgh with a truck filled with merchandise. When I got to Pittsburgh, I met up with people who were making Pittsburgh shirts and bags. It happened to be right around Christmastime—perfect timing. I found someone who was running a holiday pop-up shop and started selling clothing.

I killed it.

I took the money I made at that pop-up shop and invested it in getting a storefront for myself. The store I rented was a former pet store on East Carson Street. It was in a 150-year-old building, and it was an ugly mess. The South Side of Pittsburgh was the place for college students from the many Pittsburgh universities to live, and they partied off-campus. There were too many bars and restaurants and coffee shops to count along East Carson Street, but no boutiques. I had a vision for my store; I sold jeans, coats, sweaters, and Pittsburgh T-shirts. Since I was so into surfing, the store also had a real surfer vibe to it.

Leanne

Now that I think about it, we grew up in freezing-cold Pittsburgh, yet we were both fascinated by surf culture. I wonder why!

Steve

I named the store Decade. I decided to live there while I was fixing it up. Even though everyone told me that opening a store would be a very risky venture, living in the store essentially *lowered* my risk because I didn't have to spend money on an apartment. I'm lucky to have the skills to fix up my own place.

Not going to lie: operating Decade was scary. It was a huge run on my credit card. Luckily, it was well received, and I was able to keep up with my bills.

"Are you sure you should do this?" the family said.

There weren't many private boutiques in Pittsburgh. Hopefully, we'll see more. I wanted to create a space that I could identify with here in town. The store had a similar design vibe to Leanne's style: white painted-brick walls, black ceiling, white floor, clean merchandising.

When I really think about it, installing Decade was one of my first big renovation jobs. I bought old doors from demolished houses at Construction Junction, a salvage store in Pittsburgh. I lined the twenty-foot ceiling with the doors. Thankfully, I had many, many friends who pitched in to help with this project.

I thought Decade was the coolest shop in the South Side, and so did everyone, including my family. For me it was not only my business but also the center of my social life. We would have bands playing and lots of parties right there in my storefront.

Around this time, my friends and I started our moped gang. I guess you can say that when I get into a hobby, I become obsessed, because once I got one moped, I wanted to buy a *whole bunch more*. I scoured Craigslist for mopeds and started collecting them. I bought every moped I could find—and they were pretty cheap too, about $100 each. My friends and I would bring them back to the store, and we'd get them running again.

Ed Zeiler and I have about ten mopeds between the two of us. It was a funny sight to see: me, a six-foot-five guy, on this tiny little moped. It was like a circus. Ed would fix the mopeds, souping them up. A moped usually goes about twenty miles an hour; Ed got it running to fifty miles an hour. (Don't try this at home, kids.) We had so much fun riding around town on those little mopeds that we named ourselves the "Dead Boys Steel City Moped Crew." I even sold T-shirts out of the store.

I was into motorcycles also, so eventually when we got tired of hunching our bodies over on those little mopeds, we moved on to motorcycles. Not as hard on my back! I eventually sold most of the mopeds—about eight of them. Anything to make a buck. It was a good time!

Mom was doing some research about our family history based on family memories, and she found out that my great-great-grandfather, Paul Fallert, had a photography studio at 1405 East Carson Street in the 1800s and into the early 1900s. I opened Decade in 2007, at 1407 East Carson Street, just one door away from my grandfather's former photography studio. I was amazed by the coincidence. The Fallert

Photography Studio was a well-known Pittsburgh photography studio, and we have since found old photos with the Fallert name stamped in gold. To be in touch with my family roots like that was so cool. It made me feel like I was in the right place at the right time.

There were a lot of things I loved about owning Decade, but one of my favorite things was making window displays. I loved the creativity of it. And I guess I did a pretty good job at it because it attracted Keith Keegan, who was vice president of marketing and creative director for American Eagle, and a member of his team, creative director Brad Shaffer. Their headquarters is in Pittsburgh. Keith really liked my window displays. They started hiring me, asking me to build window displays. They would come up with concepts on paper, and I would build them. It was a great side business for me that turned into something even bigger, because word got around the American Eagle office that I could create anything.

It was a great freelance gig—all because of my store. Then other opportunities came up; other clothing brands hired me, like ModCloth, a vintage-inspired store in Pittsburgh, and rue21, another local retail brand. My name got around. Gotta love word-of-mouth marketing.

Decade, my store, was open for ten years. (Yes, ironically, a decade.) It opened a lot of doors for me. I met a ton of people, made lots of connections. People came in, we'd become friends, and then I'd work for them, like what happened with American Eagle. Most days I'd sit on the street in a chair, just hanging out, and I'd meet people in the neighborhood and invite them into the store. This was my *entire* life for ten years. Owning and running that store kept me creative and fluid, and it made me realize that I liked being visual.

I closed the store after ten years because what Leanne and I were doing was getting bigger and bigger. Financially, working with Leanne was more profitable than owning Decade, with all of its overhead.

While I wouldn't necessarily call the store profitable, I wouldn't consider it a failure. It was an experience that opened so many other doors.

It is important in business to be flexible. My customers, family, and friends were all sad to see Decade close. We had a lot of good times there, and a lot of retail happiness for all. I may reopen it someday. We'll see.

But what I learned from owning Decade is about developing my passion. It was part of *who I was.* Look: a lot of times in your life you have to take a job to get a paycheck. You have to make money, so you take the job. But I wanted more than a job. I wanted a challenge.

This doesn't mean that you'll be worry-free following a passion. I always worry a little bit. Now I worry about budgets. My only worry is budgets—and how to get things done on time, and if everyone is happy. I'm worried right now writing this book! I'm worried I'm not going to be able to meet my general contractor Bobby Benson at the house we're working on tonight to finish the job.

Leanne

What does it mean to take a risk? Does it mean you think you're going to fail?

Adam Grant, author of *Originals*—an incredible book that I've marked with underlining in so many places—did an enormous amount of research about original thinkers and people who take risks. "Originals feel fear, too," he explained in a TED talk from 2016. "They're afraid of failing, but what sets them apart from the rest of us is they're even *more* afraid of failing to try. They know you can fail by starting a business that goes bankrupt or by failing to start a business at all. They know that in the long run, our biggest regrets are not our actions but our inactions.

I definitely cut my own bangs here (and am still doing it too). I guess I knew my signature look early on! Shout-out to our cane chairs and jungle wallpaper.

Still have those bangs—and that stage presence!

I liked school that day.

Sporty Steve.

Our happy childhood home, where most of our favorite memories were made.

Steve and me trying to swing dance on my sixteenth birthday. He dropped me on my head immediately after this was taken. Don't worry, I'm fine!

The Ford kids hit the slopes. (Early 90s, anyone?)

Every summer our whole family went to Deer Valley YMCA family camp in the mountains of western Pennsylvania.

Ford Family Archives

Dad always loved getting all of us into that sailboat for a cruise on Deer Valley Lake.

Ford Family Archives

Happy times! We sure did laugh a lot.

Ford Family Archives

Hitting the open road on one of my eleven trips driving cross-country.

At Salvation Mountain working on a photo shoot for *Foam* magazine the day I adopted Tom Ford.

Tom Ford and me sitting in the apartment I lived in above Steve's place.

Ford Family Archives
Surfing with the
Pittsburgh Bridge
in the background.

Leanne and me in front of
my shop, Decade.
Ford Family Archives

Ford Family Archives
I sold those shirts at Decade.
The finished project seen in
this photo was later featured
in *Domino* magazine.

(*Right*) Erik is pretty much the best decision I've ever made. This was a very, very good day.

Sarah Barlow

(*Below*) There's nothing more wonderful than sitting with my new husband at a gorgeous table surrounded with love from our beautiful family. We appreciated every second of that evening.

Sarah Barlow

Alexandra Ribar

The "after" of the project we did for our HGTV pilot. Lots of blood, sweat, and tears went into this project, but it got us our show!

Ford Family Archives

The entire crew from season 1 of *Restored by the Fords*.

Ford Family Archives

Some incredible ladies from my design team helping Steve and me pull off yet another rushed project.

Hey, Leanne! Let's take a break and have a photo shoot! Having this opportunity to make a TV show with my little sister has been so incredible.

Steve and me still smiling somehow, despite exhaustion from many late nights prepping for the big reveal of this dreamy cottage.

The things we wish we could redo, if you look at the science, are the chances *not* taken."[2]

What's the worst that could happen? You need to weigh that risk. Can you lose money? Lose sleep? Lose peace of mind? Or is it simpler? Is it the fear of failure?

This doesn't mean that your twenties are the only time you can take a risk. It certainly makes it easier if you don't have any responsibilities tying you down; that is true. But it's just as scary, and sometimes even more crucial, to take a big leap of faith when you're older.

Truth be told: our mom is in the same house we grew up since I was born. There's a stability to that, which I think has given both of us a concept of safety. I also think Steve and I were able to run around the country and move to all these places because we knew we'd have her house to go back to if any plan backfired. Maybe that's what gave me the courage to move to Nashville, despite everyone's protests, despite it being a wild card.

Moving to Nashville ended up being a tremendous success because that was where I needed to be in my life at that time. Living in Nashville was *my* choice, *my* risk. It was about me jumping into my career and jumping into a quality of life because that's what I craved. It was the time in my life that I was really able to get creative in the fashion world, and to do it in Nashville was a dream. Enjoy living in the moment— even if it means a potential for failure.

Steve

As much fun as I had in California, moving back to Pittsburgh was one of the best things I've ever done—just like creating Decade. I like that there's no traffic here. (Or less traffic, I should say.) The cost of living is lower than in California. It made it easier to do the things that I liked. Here, my bills are easier to pay.

After living nine months in the back of the store, using my Murphy bed, my garden hose as a shower, and a Pittsburgh potty in the basement, I finally moved to the apartment above my store that became available after the neighbors moved out. (That may or may not have been because of my late-night parties.)

Leanne

I have always stayed connected to Pittsburgh and always will. It's where my family is; therefore, it's where my heart is.

I moved back to Pittsburgh from Nashville and lived above Steve's apartment. I wasn't there for even a year, but that didn't stop me from fully decorating it. I painted the old, beat-up wood floors white and ripped out the dumpy old uppers in the kitchen. I used old fabric I had as wallpaper down the hall and filled the place with thrift-store finds and hand-me-downs. I had a desk looking out the window over the South Side of Pittsburgh, and I would sit there and type out songs and poems on my old typewriter.

I always think about Dad's favorite book, *Acres of Diamonds*, by the founder of Temple University, Russell H. Conwell. Conwell's philosophy was simple: you can find everything you need for your success in your own backyard.

Conwell tells one story I'll never forget, about a wealthy Persian farmer. Maybe you've heard it? He had learned that his country was filled with diamonds and became obsessed with finding them; he wanted wealth and would do anything to obtain it. So he sold off his farm, and off he went in search of diamonds. He spent his entire life trekking around, looking for these precious stones, traveling to Palestine, to Europe, until he got to Spain, where he gave up on everything and threw himself into a river. He died hopeless, penniless, and alone.

Meanwhile, the man he sold his farm to was out taking a leisurely walk. He saw a flash of light in his garden brook and reached down into the water. He lifted up a black stone with a tiny sparkle, illuminating all of the colors of the rainbow. He thought it was so pretty that he took the stone into his house and put it on his mantel to enjoy. His friend came over to the house, saw the stone, and said, "Do you know what that is?"

It was a diamond. In fact, that farm turned out to be one of the largest diamond mines on the continent. The poor, misguided man who had sold it off in his quest for riches forgot to look in his own backyard.[3]

I loved the adventures of my years in New York, LA, and Nashville. I still spend a lot of time in all those cities. I learned so much about myself and about what I want my life to be. But it turns out that my hometown of Pittsburgh would be the place the *big* stuff in my life would happen. It's where Steve and I would start working together, which would set us on a path that we still have trouble believing is real at times. Pittsburgh is where I bought my one-hundred-year-old schoolhouse, which launched my decorating career. This is the place where Steve and I renovate homes for so many people and, through the magic of television, give millions of others ideas of how to make their spaces beautiful too.

Steve

Pittsburgh is steeped in history, which is pretty cool. Sometimes when I take a back road to my place, I wind up the hilly streets, looking at all the public staircases that weave their way through the terrain. I think about how the steelworkers would trudge up those steps, up through the hills to go home. Our grandparents worked hard in these hills to get their families to a better place in life. And then I think about Dad, and how proud of us he would have been.

Leanne

Yep. Dad would have been thrilled that we were here, filming our show in Pittsburgh. Right here, as Conwell preached, in our own backyard, renovating houses together and giving people a home that they love.

Steve

The only thing I really missed about California when I moved back home was the surfing. So I figured out how to surf right here in Pittsburgh.

I know. Those two words, *surf* and *Pittsburgh*, don't exactly go together.

But I'm not your average person. I look at life a little differently than everyone else.

I love the water. I love how it feels to be free. Making time to get out to where where I feel close to nature is so important for my soul. You have to do what you love and make time for yourself; for me, that's wakesurfing.

At Decade, I talked about surfing with many of my customers, since the store had a real California surfer vibe to it. I knew people in a landlocked state like Pennsylvania were going to be interested in wakesurfing.

The Monongahela River runs right through Pittsburgh, and it's clean here. It's not a lake, but it's a great option for wakesurfing. Hey, work with what you've got, right?

A friend first introduced wakesurfing to me in 2002. The sport is similar to waterskiing, except you're not on skis. You're on a board. We actually spend more time on a nine-foot-six nose rider than on the smaller boards. As with waterskiing, you need a rope to get going, but once you catch the wake of the boat, you let the rope go. You surf right behind the wake, and sometimes the wake can reach four feet. It's pretty incredible.

Wakesurfing boats are made especially so that they sit extremely low in the water without sinking. Because you're trailing closely behind the boat in wakesurfing, the prop is in the *middle* of the boat—a lot safer.

A special wakesurfing boat costs about $40,000. And guess what? I didn't have $40,000.

Because I like to try to work my way out of every tough situation, and because I never really give up, I bought a $5,000 boat and tried to turn it into a wakesurfing boat. I called it the *Werewolf*, because it roared.

Nothing was going to stop me from surfing on that river. The *Werewolf* was so fast—so fast that it would turn on a dime. If I turned it hard enough, and if you were on it, you'd fall off the back of it. You need slow for wakesurfing. You need torque—power, not speed.

But that's not all you need; you need the back of the boat to sink down into the water without it filling up with water. I know—tricky. And I couldn't sink this boat deep enough. Some friends and I tried. We had a one-thousand-pound bag of water weighing the boat down, but we still couldn't make it happen. The bag of water sank the boat— you've seen the movie *Titanic*. I needed a boat that would create a wave, not a boat that would sink to the bottom of the river.

So how could I get the $40,000 wakesurfing boat? I had a new plan. I'd start a wakesurfing business, and teaching lessons on the weekends would pay for the boat. I loved teaching people how to wakesurf. It was so much fun. That was enough to convince me—that was the plan. I sold the *Werewolf*, bought a wakesurfing boat, and named her *Simply Business*.

I launched Surf Pittsburgh, and people became as interested as I knew they would be. A lot of people in the business district flocked to it. Imagine how cool it would be to come out of your building after work and hop in the river to surf. Yeah, it's pretty cool.

Of course, at first people were surprised. They would see us on the river with the boat and someone spinning in the waves. People would just stand there and stare, eyes wide open, like, *What on earth is that?*

At first, maybe I'd see one other person wakesurfing in Pittsburgh. But then, a year later, I saw six other people doing it. One of my clients wanted to go out on the water every Friday. He used to do golf trips on Fridays, and now he just wanted to do wakesurfing. He'd bring a whole crew with him, and I'd pick him up downtown after work.

I ran Surf Pittsburgh for three years—taking people out on the boat and giving them experiences they enjoyed. And I loved it! But, again, the overhead cost more than my earnings, so Surf Pittsburgh became a happy memory.

I had lots of fun and connected with people who are still part of my life today. I still have a boat, and I surf as much as possible. It was just another "failure" that's not a failure in my book.

If you're afraid to fail, you're going to be stuck. You're never going to experiment. You're never going to try. You're never going to surf!

I think people expect success too quickly; they put such high expectations on themselves. Instead of writing challenges off as failures, think of them as *experiments*. It's all a part of what makes us who we are. It's about living on purpose.

Leanne

We Fords are resilient, aren't we? Steve and I have had multiple careers—and we'll probably have more.

People seem to think that they have to have it all figured out by a certain age, but life doesn't work that way. We need to leave space in our lives to evolve. We are works in progress. And for progress to happen, you have to let that process happen. And if that means starting a company where you teach people how to surf on the river in Pittsburgh—then cool, go for it.

WORKING ON PROGRESS

Is there anything you've always wanted to do that you haven't done yet? Is there any way you can do it now? Even temporarily?

Have you found something to love that adds joy to your life?

You don't need to leave everything to start something new. What can you do and create right where you are with what you have?

What are the opportunities you have in your own backyard that you are overlooking?

Whom can you help as they are looking to create opportunities in their own backyard?

In the simplest form, what makes you happy? How can you do more of that?

8

Roam on Home

*Remember this, that if you wish to be great at all,
you must begin where you are and what you are.*

—RUSSELL HERMAN CONWELL

Leanne

People ask me how I got into design. Honestly, it's all because of one pretty little bathroom.

Let me backtrack a little. In 2010, I moved back to Pittsburgh and found an amazing old schoolhouse, the one I talked about earlier, located about thirty minutes outside of the city. It was a run-down place and needed a lot of work, but I was inspired because I had been dying to rip down some walls and reconfigure a space. When you really own something, you can do that. You don't have to ask a landlord for approval.

Fashion was still my bread and butter. I had been styling people for years at this point. When I bought my schoolhouse, I knew the renovation would be a challenge, but I had no idea how inspired I'd be by decorating. All of a sudden, I had a vision, and I had a blank canvas.

One of the bigger visions and harder to-dos was to renovate the upstairs bathroom. It was a tiny little bathroom, which started out as nothing special at all. There was a slanted roof. There was a tiny window that looked bad from the inside and outside; you know—a dinky little shower window with no natural light. It was bad. But the biggest problem I had to figure out was where to fit a bathtub. This was my A-number-one priority. I was definitely putting a bathtub in that room. No was not an option. I take a bath every day—sometimes twice, if I'm lucky!

Up to this point, my then husband, my friends, my family, and I had done everything ourselves. But we were exhausted, so I decided to do it the "real" way: I called a contractor. Someone came in from a large contracting company. I told him my idea: I wanted white subway tiles. A big open shower with no curtains. No glass. An octagon-tiled floor and a tub underneath the slanted roof, right there in the shower.

"You can't do that. I've never seen that."

Now, you know I don't take no for an answer. I've been this way since I was ten years old and painting Mom's refrigerator.

So I spoke to two more contractors. They all said the same thing: "You can't do that, I've never seen that before."

I can't tell you how frustrating that was. I had a vision. The vision was clear. And I had spent so many years implementing my vision in the fashion world. Now here were these three people telling me I couldn't do it, just because they said they'd never seen it before. Please.

So I was going to figure it out without them. That's when I called Steve.

Steve

And I took the job. Because, you know, the price was right and she needed help. So I called my friends and made them come over and figured it out. We worked, but it felt more like a party. It was a fun job.

Leanne

Yeah, I paid them in beer, pretty much. I always had beer and tequila there—drinks upon arrival for Steve and his friends. When they'd leave after working on my house, they'd say "Thanks. We had a great time!" Or they'd say after a long day's work, "We got to go home soon, Leanne," and I would hand them another drink, and they'd stay there for another couple of hours. I'm no fool!

But basically, Steve didn't have a choice. No one else would work on it.

Steve

I'm not going to lie: I felt the same way that the contractors felt. I stepped into that house and I thought, *How are we going to do this?*

The space was tricky. It was an old house. Everything was a little bit iffy. Everything was outdated, and it needed a ton of work. But anything that Leanne wants is a little trickier than what your average human being wants. It's a little more of a MacGyver situation. But in the end, it's always a little better and more interesting her way.

It's that little tweak that Leanne puts on something. It's that push that she takes to make it jump to the next level. I really respect that about her.

Leanne

I'm going to have to remind you that you wrote that, Steve, when you're mad at me *during* the process. I'll just show you this book the next time you complain about my ideas. Because it's no fail: every single time I have an idea on the show, he complains about it. And then, like clockwork, every time we do a reveal, he says, "This actually looks really good."

I have an idea, Steve. What if we take out that in-between, where you're complaining, and it's just a nice, lovely experience?

Steve

Here's the thing: my thought process is probably a lot like Dad's. Remember the time Leanne and Mom painted the avocado refrigerator white? I'm sure Dad liked it once it was done, but his first instinct was to mull it over, or just right off the bat say no. Because who paints a refrigerator?

Dad was a cautious guy. And even though it might not seem like I'm careful because of all the extreme sports I dive into, I'm actually supercautious about my decision-making. I don't want it to seem like I'm complaining or shutting Leanne down while we're working on the shot—because obviously Leanne has amazing ideas!—but I just need a little time to figure it all out. Unfortunately, when we're shooting the television show, the pace is so fast. We have to make decisions, like, boom-boom-boom. I could probably use a little more time to allow that mental process to happen.

Leanne

If I'm the MacGyver of design, Steve is the MacGyver of construction. His problem is *he figures it out*. If he didn't figure it out, I wouldn't keep asking him to do weird stuff. Poor guy.

Which is what happened with my bathroom. He—along with an amazing crew of guys—helped me figure it out.

Right next to the existing bathroom was a crawl space and a massive closet taking up space. That was all I needed. I wanted it all gone so I had extra room to play with.

I think the reason that I am good at design is because I see it differently. Steve actually said this once, which I loved: "Leanne doesn't just think outside the box; she rips the box down." I start over. I see the potential in everything, which was a problem in dating, but great in renovating houses.

So we did it: we broke into the crawl space and lost the massive bathroom closet. We put the bathtub under the slanted roof, which was another "problem," according to contractors. "You won't be able to stand up in your bathtub," they said.

"Who needs to stand up in their bathtub?" I replied.

To deal with the light, I put this *massive* full-size window in the shower. Another "no-can-do" from the contractors I spoke to.

"You can't put a window in your shower that big," they said. That's a privacy issue.

To solve that problem, I hung *outdoor shutters* on the inside of the shower. They are, after all, meant to be completely weatherproof. It was perfect because I could close them when I needed privacy and open them up when I wanted natural light.

Steve

Most people's brains don't work the way our brains work. Genetically, our brains are similar, which is great in a lot of ways, especially when we're working together. (It can also be terrible in a lot of ways.) Yesterday, for instance, we walked in and told the clients, "The bathroom has to move from one side of the house to the other." It was a no-brainer. But the clients were stunned. Move a bathroom?

Just because a house was built a particular way doesn't mean it's the *right* way. And it also doesn't mean it has to *stay* that way.

Leanne had other thoughts for changes to her schoolhouse. She wanted to expose the beams in her kitchen. She knew that her ceiling had to go, so she would take a hammer to it and try to knock things down on her own. She's determined, but you've probably figured that out already.

Her bathroom was a fun, challenging project. It was fun because it was Leanne's, and it did feel in a way like we were playing, like making forts again. Except this time, I was helping Leanne build *her* own fort. (Me and a crew of people and friends. Of course, you cannot do this kind of work by yourself, no matter how it looks on television.) She was busy running around the country, working on her styling jobs, and I would FaceTime her as I was tearing the ceiling out.

"Are you sure this is what you want, Leanne?"

"Yes, tear it out!"

She was a great client, actually, when I look back at it. That's right; I saw her as a client. I did what she wanted, but she also gave me a little room and trusted me, so I got to do a few things I wanted.

Working with Leanne is challenging, yes, but it's the opposite of boring. It's the opposite of hanging drywall; it's more creative. With Leanne, it's all about texture. I could understand her vision, and it was fun to make it happen.

You know how you go into a restaurant and there's a vibe? It's the same thing with homes. When you walk into a house Leanne's decorated, it has a life of its own. I like to be part of that creative process.

Also, I really respected that when Leanne decided to design her own home, she couldn't care less what people thought about it.

"I'm gonna make this house look like *this*. Because that's what *I* want it to look like. I don't need everyone to like it; I need to do what I love for it," she said. That was really her motto.

Obviously when we're taking on clients, that's different. We cater to what the client wants.

Leanne

Yes, because as a designer, my most important thing is to make the client happy.

But this time, I was the client. I was my *first* client, in fact.

Renovating the bathroom was definitely hard, but now I had this gorgeous bathroom. If I designed within the *couldn't-shouldn't-wouldn't, nobody's ever done it* mentality, then *none* of these designs would exist. Neither would my newest career path.

We worked on this house for two years. My first husband did most of the labor with Steve and his friends, which I will forever appreciate. But the aesthetics were really mine. (I had designed everywhere I've lived since I was ten years old.) Lose a wall here; lose a ceiling; redo the layout. It was my first time, a total learning experience.

Around that time, I started writing a blog about my house and the bathroom. I'm pretty sure the only person who read the blog was Mom. Well, Mom and Jordan Barnes. Jordan, a friend of mine I worked with at a magazine, showed the blog to the editor of *Country Living*, my favorite magazine. And they called! I couldn't believe it. They wanted to shoot *my* house and that bathroom.

While I was waiting for the *Country Living* spread to come out, my friend Alexandra, who owns a jewelry line called Sabika with her family, happened to open new offices and asked me to design them for her.

"I have never done this before," I told Alexandra. "But I'll do it if you're okay with me practicing on you. You know I'll be making it up as I go along."

She and her family were the greatest clients. They let me try out different design ideas; I got to see what worked and what didn't—and in the end, they were so happy.

"I give people the tour and walk them around," Alexandra told me. "People tell us, 'This is so Sabika. This place is so you.' And we just wink," she said. That's still one of my favorite design compliments.

About a year later, when the *Country Living* article came out, the phone calls started coming in. People wanted to hire me. One of my first clients from the *Country Living* spread was a woman named Kelly. She knew I was local. She knew I was a newbie. And she wanted me to design her house.

I was completely overwhelmed.

"I'll call you right back," I said to her.

I called one of my favorite friends since childhood, Danny Mazzarini, who lives and works in New York. "How do I become an interior designer? What do I do? How much do I charge? How do I translate my brain and design ideas to a finished product?"

Danny spent about two hours on the phone with me, going through every detail. That was my schooling. He told me what to charge, what I should present to the client. He told me that I could create a design board just the way I would when I was styling for someone. He told me where to get furniture. It would be an easy transition, because the truth is, there are so many similarities between fashion and design.

I could do it.

I called her back and said, "I'll do it!"

The budget was nothing. We did Kelly's whole first floor and kitchen for $20,000. We painted the cabinets and reused as much as we could. We built shelves instead of uppers. I went to IKEA and sample sales. Steve and Ed helped on that job. Kelly was living there through all of the work, yet, ironically enough, she asked me to do a reveal for her.

"Let's pretend this is like an HGTV show," she said. So she left for the day as I installed the furniture and made the finishing touches.

When she came home and saw it, she cried.

She was so thrilled. The redesign just breathed new life into her house.

Now she's really into design, and she takes risks. She always moves her furniture around. It literally changed her life, having a home she loved. She's still a friend and one of my biggest supporters.

And it all started from my little bathroom, the bathroom that no one wanted to renovate.

At the same time, my career as a stylist had evolved as the years had gone by, and I was being brought in by clothing companies to help with creative direction. I was in charge of the photo shoots for many large brands, which meant I would pitch them the vision of the shoot, pick the photographer and crew that would best translate the vision, find the location, choose the models, style the looks, and so on. On set I would give directions of where to shoot which model for which look. This work required me to use so many different parts of my brain and the instincts that I had developed over the years. The details are what make the image—or in my case now, the room—or whatever you are working on special. I applied my taste for looks that are slightly undone to my work as a creative director, just as I apply those instincts to the work I do now designing homes with a casual, lived-in feel.

My life as a creative director took me all over the world. It was the perfect job for me at a perfect time in my career. I was fulfilled creatively, I made my own schedule, and I was able to travel to places I would have never seen otherwise. My five years of work in the field gave me the financial security to buy that little schoolhouse and then the little farmhouse that I fixed up in Pittsburgh, which was featured in *Domino* magazine.

Going from fashion to interiors was an amazing transition that I couldn't have planned if I wanted to. But my creative brain was starting to get confused. I would be on set in some exotic location, trying to help a client decide between the two light fixtures I was pitching to them. I was overextending myself, and it was time for me to make a decision about the direction of my career: Do I stay with what I know or do I leave a successful career to dive headfirst into a new career that isn't guaranteed?

I had to consciously let go of what I knew worked for me to head off into the unknown. But you know what? It wasn't even a contest for me. Interior design was inspiring and exciting and renewing, and it was calling loud and clear. It was time to answer the phone.

It's an amazing thing about the universe: when you say, "Here I am; this is what I am doing," and you stop dipping your toes in the water and jump, it works. The people around you see your intentions, and they want to help you. Most people are loving and supportive, and they want you to do well and excel.

Once I told people I was doing interior design, the world opened up to me. People passed my name on to friends, they passed my work on to editors, and those people are why you are reading this book right now. What a beautiful thing.

WORKING ON PROGRESS

Who do you know who is trying to pursue a new passion? How can you encourage them? Help them? Who can you introduce them to? You have no idea the snowball effect you could be giving someone with a simple word of encouragement or connection.

9

I Want My HGTV

My advice, Daisy, is to go as far in
life as God and luck allow.

—MRS. HUGHES, *DOWNTON ABBEY*

Leanne

We have a TV show right now. Forgive me if what I am about to say sounds messed up, but . . . so then what? Fame is fickle; glory is fleeting. But talent and drive are yours to keep. And what you add to the universe will stay here in some way. Your creative life, your love, how you treat your family—those things stick. Your job might go away, your relationship might go away, but your inherent talent isn't going away. Even when you yourself do go away, make sure you leave something here for those behind you. Inspire people around you to live fuller, more joyfully, more fearlessly. Inspire others to create without boundaries or concern of success, to love without worry about tomorrow. Work hard today. Love hard today.

I had never intended to be in front of the camera. I had always been a really shy kid, actually. My sister, Michelle, would say that I never spoke to anyone except for Mom.

"Half the time she was on Mom's leg," Michelle says. "Not scared, but definitely not interested in talking to anyone."

When we had babysitters, apparently, I'd stand in the corner, crying because Mom was gone.

When I would go all quiet, my grandma would say, "Leanne's thinking." I guess I was saving it up, because I grew out of that, to say the least. I'm certainly not shy now. And I'm strangely fine being in front of a camera. (That doesn't mean I have to watch it, though!)

The schoolhouse, the Sabika office, and Kelly's home were the only interior design projects I had done, but it was a really exciting time for me. Working on my own house was really thrilling. That blog I wrote never went anywhere. (I never even meant for it to; it was mainly for our family.) But turns out that little blog had two very important readers: Natalie Warady of *Country Living*, and Peter Barbee.

Peter, who has a band, Among Savages (an awesome band, by the way), had a friend, Lindsey Weidhorn, who was looking for new talent for HGTV. Specifically, they were scouting for a cute couple who liked to fix up homes together for a brand-new show.

Peter told his friend at HGTV all about what we were doing at the schoolhouse; he also told his friend about me and my first husband. But my first husband wasn't interested, so we didn't pursue it. I don't actually know if HGTV said no to us or we said no to them in this round; there's plenty of *no* in this story, so you'll understand why I can't remember. After some Skyping and such, we parted ways amicably and respectfully.

But we didn't part ways before I told the network, "Just FYI. I do a lot of work with my brother. Let me know if that's ever of interest to you."

And that was that. The HGTV talk just went away.

I was totally fine and happy to carry on my way. I had just started my design career, and I needed more time to know what I was doing, to hone my craft. Those years between that first discussion and actually being on TV really allowed me to sink deeper into becoming a designer. It allowed me to build a reputation in my field.

I am thankful to have come into the world of HGTV with an established career as an interior designer. I consider myself an interior designer first and foremost; I don't consider myself a TV personality. TV is secondary to what I do creatively, to my true passion of design. And when the show goes away, I will still be out here making something or other somewhere or other.

In fact, I don't think I even told Steve that I ever mentioned his name. I don't think I told him about it at all. It was so off-the-cuff, a quick sentence in an email, and off I went about my business.

Steve

Nope! I had no idea.

Leanne

I guess I didn't tell you because it felt like too much of a pipe dream. A show on HGTV? How far off in the stars is that concept?

Having a TV show is not anything that I could have even locked my mind onto. It wasn't anything that I could even visualize. It felt very far away. To this day I still marvel and sometimes say out loud, "We have a TV show?"

About a year later, in 2014, I got a call from HGTV, and they wanted to speak to me again. They wanted to film what's called in the television world a "sizzle." A sizzle is about a three- to five-minute, fast-paced video that gives an idea of what the show is going to be about. It's a pretty standard video so that the producers at HGTV can get a feel for who the talent is and what the premise of the show would be.

At that point, I was renovating a Pittsburgh farmhouse, so I thought it would be the perfect spot to film. The house was built in 1940. I added wide wood boards to all the ceilings, leaving cracks between the boards so the lights we installed behind them would glow through the cracks. We added wood to the walls and painted them white. The walls I didn't paint got ripped out. I used beautiful antique and brass touches that I found in Mexico and Paris. I brought in Moroccan rugs and lights to play off of the industrial warehouse lights I had found around Pittsburgh. I used an old Hobie sail as a shower curtain (an ode to my days as camp counselor). The master bathroom doors were old Craigslist finds that I had held on to for years, just waiting for the right project. I designed and built the bathroom *and* walls around those $200 doors.

In the guest bathroom, I used an old tub that had come from a friend's house. I commissioned a magical spiral-style raw wood staircase from our buddy Ed Zeiler, replacing the drop-down stairs from the attic. That staircase renovation allowed us to create an entirely new space to live in. I exposed the rafters in the attic and painted everything white. Goodbye, attic. Hellllllo, dream office.

"My brother's helping me renovate my farmhouse," I told the HGTV producer. "Maybe you can come film us working on that?" They loved that idea.

It was winter, and I had my big fur coat on. I also wore oversized round sunglasses, which I still wear, by the way. One might say that I looked like a cross between Diane Keaton and the ninety-seven-year-old fashion icon Iris Apfel. Which might not have been the look HGTV was going for. Oh! And my hair was rock 'n' roll blonde. Maybe I was a little too quirky for them.

Soon after, I got an email from Katie Neff, a producer who had helped develop *Fixer Upper*. "Unfortunately, the consensus is that you're too 'hip, fabulous and cool' for HGTV," she wrote in the email.

Too cool? Not something I am often accused of, really. Was it the glasses?

HGTV wasn't interested in a show around me, my farmhouse, my scrappy brother, and my big sunglasses.

"All good, Katie," I wrote back. "Thank you so much for letting me know. If you're going to get denied, at least it's for being too cool. Listen, I'm here. Call me when you're ready."

I remember thinking, *I'm not going anywhere. And my style isn't that crazy! Your viewers will catch up. There are a lot of us—people who like neutrals. People who like to wear . . . interesting outfits.*

I knew that I personally wanted to see more people with my aesthetic on television. People who like black houses and white walls.

We are out here. And we love looking at design!

I left the window open, but I closed the door on that chapter, thinking, *Well, HGTV is just not in the cards.* And you know what? That was *fine.* That the idea of an HGTV show was even a *glimmer* of a glimmer of a glimmer of a possibility was wild. An absolute thrill.

With that sweet but simple email, I closed my computer and went back to . . . oh, I don't know—painting something, I'm sure.

It was a time for new beginnings. By that time my first husband and I had sadly but lovingly parted ways, and I threw myself into my passion for design. It restored me; it was where I found so much joy. I built up my portfolio. I took on clients and created fresh, new aesthetics for their homes. More and more press opportunities and requests started coming in. That was amazing—it was so good for my career. I really needed that time, I realized. I had become known to some of my favorite editors and magazines and in certain small design circles. If HGTV had worked out earlier, I might not have known who I really was as a designer. I didn't want to be a TV personality who was learning the ropes about the design world. I wanted to be an experienced designer who *happened* to have a TV show.

I wasn't in *any* way banking on, planning on, or pining over a television show for myself.

That's when the production company with HGTV emailed us. Again. For the third time!

They came back to me and pretty much said, "Well, it's not dead yet!" They kept reviving and evolving that original pitch video. Unbeknownst to me, they'd mention our names, pitch us again, and then get shut down. Then the cycle would start all over again. Someone would say, "What about Leanne Ford?" God bless whoever that person was! They just kept bringing it back and championing us, which I appreciate so much.

Finally, Katie Neff from High Noon production company contacted me because they wanted to pitch me again. It was 2015. This time they wanted to do a brand-new sizzle. You know: give a fresh look. It had been almost two years since the last one, after all.

"They want us to re-Skype you and your brother for a new format that they think you guys could be perfect for," Katie wrote in an email. "Which makes me VERY HAPPY!"

And then Katie wrote: "Oh, Leanne. Don't wear your fur coat *[Smiley face.]*"

They set up a three-way Skype interview. Katie Neff was in her office. I was in Los Angeles, sitting in the family room. Steve was in Pittsburgh, drinking a beer in his garage. Yes, this is how the Ford family does an interview.

Steve

I had a Koozie on over the beer.

Leanne

Doesn't change the fact that it was a still a beer, Steve.

It was such a fun conversation. I actually had a great time.

"Katie, can you come around all the time?" I said to her at the end of the conversation. "My brother talks so much more when you're here!"

We all cheered to each other over Skype. Here's to a great television show in our future! After we hung up, I thought, *Whoa. Steve's fun. It's the most I've ever heard Steve talk in the last fifteen years!* (But not anymore! Now we always talk.) It was nice to see him in that light and to dream about a show where we worked together. It felt right.

Katie made a pitch video out of our Skype interview along with pictures and projects we had done. And the pitch (not-so-spoiler alert!) was a hit. It made it to round two.

Steve

I really was shocked. This wasn't anything I ever pursued. I never thought that I wanted to be on TV or be in the public eye. Leanne was always way more comfortable than me in front of people. Her design layouts and renovations were taking off, and I was super happy for her. But for me, I was perfectly content to be in the background. I was just hanging out, doing my job.

Next thing I knew, Leanne was saying, "Hey, want to be on a TV show with me?" And I thought, *Sure. Why not? Of course I'll do that.* I work with my sister already; why would it be so different with TV cameras around?

Leanne

It's worth noting that we spent much of our childhood in front of Dad's large, over-the-shoulder camcorder. I see videos now of us as children, and I was constantly giving commentary on what was going on, which was more often than not Steve giving a tour of his forts and making mountain-biking videos. We had plenty of practice in front of the camera together. Probably twenty years of it, to be exact.

And that was that. We went back to our normal lives. There were two big takeaways from this whole experience. One, be patient. It takes so long for anything in the entertainment industry to happen, and you are at the whim of many other people. Second, let it play out naturally. I wasn't worried or stressed about whether this was going to happen or not. *If this is going to happen,* I thought, *it's going to happen. And if it's not supposed to—it's not going to.* I really believed that and still do.

I always say, "Thy will be done." For me, this means that God's got a better plan than any plan I could dream up. I say life is pretty much this simple: Make plans. Adjust accordingly. Go with the supernatural flow.

My husband, Erik, said to me once, "It's no wonder you're so confident. Because you don't gain your worth from any earthly source." I liked that observation.

Shortly after the sizzle went to HGTV, I went to Palm Springs with Erik. We were sitting in a little restaurant for lunch. We were there soaking up the rays and the beautiful weather in Palm Springs, enjoying a little time to ourselves. I overheard a man at the table next to me talking about cabinetry. A favorite subject of mine, as you might guess.

A couple of minutes later, the man got up and approached our table.

"I'm so sorry to interrupt you," he said with a big, friendly smile. "Are you Leanne Ford?"

"Yes," I said.

"I just had to say hi. I've watched your sizzle about twenty times, and I love you and your brother. I'm Loren Ruch from HGTV."

Loren Ruch is the group SVP of development and production at HGTV.

My heart almost stopped. Here we were, in Palm Springs, and the bigwig from HGTV was sitting next to us and recognized me.

"We watched sixty sizzles. We picked one," he said. He looked me right in the eye. "And it was yours."

I couldn't believe what I was hearing. I didn't really know the magnitude of what it all meant, but I knew it was amazing. It was divine intervention. *Hold on to your hat, lady!*

I loved talking to Loren. I didn't want him to leave! Loren has since become a very good friend to both Steve and me. He's become a huge champion for our show. He's incredibly supportive. I need to get him a "World's Best Boss" mug.

I remember walking out of that restaurant arm in arm with Erik. "It's going to happen, isn't it?" I said to him.

"Yes," Erik said. "It sure is."

———

To say we didn't know what we were getting ourselves into would be an understatement. And to be honest, that might have been for the best. Looking back, I'm glad we were oblivious to the great abyss we had just jumped into. Sometimes naivete is the best tool for progress. Then again, sometimes it's not.

It felt to us as if we had hit the lottery. I mean, here we were, with a television show. We really thought everything was going to be smooth sailing from here.

Smooth sailing? Try again, girl. I had no idea what was waiting for me down the line.

It was time to film our first project: the pilot.

Steve

The only issue was me getting used to being in front of the camera. In my opinion, Leanne seemed to be a natural. Me, not as much. It was really hard for the first few weeks. But I started to get used to it all because we had such a great production team.

Leanne

What? That's not true, Steve! You had one early day where you were saying, "This is weird. This is awkward." But then the next day, all of a sudden, the camera would show up, and your voice would get lower, and you would say very *professionally*, "Okay. So we're going to need to fix this attic situation." I was cracking up.

Steve was very confident when the cameras were on, and he would say, all chipper, "Hey Leanne, I've got an idea!" Steve is *never* chipper. He was using those acting skills he got from *Dreamgirls*, I guess.

Right off the bat, at the first production meeting, the producers threw me a curveball.

"Leanne, can you do a house with some color?" the producers said.

Oh no you didn't.

If you know my work at all, you know color is a rare sighting. I have always worked with neutrals. Black and white. This isn't something that I deviate from often. I created a T-shirt that I wear on the show that reads "Wear Black, Paint White." This is what I'm known for.

Again, I was an interior designer *before* the show, and I'm going to be an interior designer *after* the show. So the last thing I wanted to do was be known for something that is not naturally authentic to my style. I couldn't produce a design that wasn't representative of who I was. I have to be true to myself, even if it's a bomb.

I figured there were two ways it could go. If I changed my style for the show and it didn't work, that would have been the worst. I was sticking to my guns. This house was going to look best in neutrals. I had to do it how I knew it needed to be done, even if it meant losing the show.

Yes, that's right—losing the show. Why? Because if you're true to yourself, you can't fail. If the show didn't work out, I'd be fine. There are plenty of things in life that don't work out, and you know what? We survive. In fact, I can pretty much promise you, we come out better because of it.

I also wanted people to see what neutrals could do for them. I wanted to teach people that white could be more than just *white*. I wanted people to know that white is, as my husband coined and I have since stolen, "the silence between the chords." It gives us the break we need from all the noise that's out there in the world.

Thankfully, the producers heard and respected my position, and we were off to the races. That's when the madness started.

Our first episode was called "Mid–Century Meets 21st Century." The clients were the Georgi family, who lived in a modern home in the country. Their budget was about $60,000. They needed a major renovation. They had some beautiful bones in the house: brick and paneling, which I loved. It just needed new life.

But here's what I quickly found out: working on a television show is completely unrelated to designing a house in real life. It's two separate entities. The producers kept saying to us, "Just do what you would do normally if we weren't here." I had to laugh. I mean, that's impossible.

Steve and I had everything invested in that pilot. We didn't know or anticipate it was going to be as much work as it turned out to be. Plumbing problems. Equipment not working. Electrical issues. Plus, a crew filming us! We had the owners move out for a couple of months— but we still didn't have enough time, and we didn't have enough help. We couldn't afford enough help! And we didn't have enough sleep. We were working all night.

Steve

Yeah, I was sleeping at that house because we were working so hard. Everyone stuck it out with me. I kept saying, "We have a deadline. We have to meet the deadline." It was like my mantra that I just kept repeating over and over again, hoping that we would actually meet that deadline.

Leanne

We jumped in so fast. We didn't have the budget set. We had a tight timetable since Steve and I had already worked together a number of times—and we have our own shorthand because we're brother and sister—but this was a totally different beast.

We didn't want to scrimp on the Georgis' house, because they were our clients—but also because it was our big shot. Our one chance. And here I was, watching this pilot unfold in total chaos. I absolutely had to pull it together. *You do this for a living*, I thought to myself. *You design beautiful homes that are shot in magazines! And now that you're doing a TV show . . . you got this.*

At a certain point, Steve and I started crumbling from the stress. It really came between the two of us.

Steve

We were fine up until the end, I guess. It just got really intense and exhausting.

Leanne

It was, for me, some serious exhaustion and tears. Steve and I find value in different things. I'm a visual person. I'm a designer. Steve is all about logistics. There was a moment in the pilot where we were sitting up in the attic, talking about the rafters. If you watch our show, or if you've seen any of my designs, you will know that I love exposed beams. It really warms up a house. But to expose the rafters in that house, Steve would have had to move all of the HVAC and the air handlers entirely. It would have cost an enormous amount of money.

Steve and I sat up there in those rafters and had a real heart-to-heart, right then and there. I wanted to expose everything. But Steve was being practical. He said to me straight up: "I see dollars just flying out the window."

"But look how good those beams look."

"Leanne, that's going to blow our $60,000 budget."

"All I see is a perfect dream ceiling," I said, because that's how I legitimately felt. Steve wanted to put all the value *behind* the walls. As a contractor, I understand that. He wants to do his job right. But we never agree on how to handle these kinds of situations.

In the end, the house came out beautiful. Steve won the ceiling debate, and we gave it a layer of gloss that brightened the space up. We painted the brick fireplace white (of course we did). Ed and Steve made a custom slab wood table. We poured our heart into every detail of this home. The master bathroom was really what pulled the owners' heartstrings. Lisa Georgi burst into tears when she saw how gorgeous it turned out: double shower, soaking tub, mahogany wall and ceiling, with tile floating to meet the wood.

Glad they loved it. 'Cause *man*, if it didn't almost kill us!

WORKING ON PROGRESS

Who can you thank for getting you to where you are today? Your parents? Your teachers? Your neighbor who encouraged you? Your college roommate? Old boss? Someone who fired you? Take a moment to thank them, whether in person, on the phone, in a letter, or even a little prayer sent their way. They deserve to know that someone out there has been encouraged or has grown by their actions or words.

10

Forever—and Then Some

Through it. In spite of it. Because of it.

—OUR VOWS

Leanne

Ever try to plan a wedding in four days?

I did. And it was my idea of perfection.

It was a Wednesday night in November, and Erik and I were staying at the Bowery Hotel in New York City. We had been newly engaged for a couple of months. Erik was opening his first New York Buck Mason store, and I was designing the space.

Here we were, on this chilly New York night, cozy in this gorgeous hotel. We were talking about *when* we wanted to get married and *where* we wanted to get married. We were just at the beginning stage of hashing it out. All we knew at this point is that we couldn't *wait* to be husband and wife.

Some brides dream of a huge wedding with hundreds of people. Not me. Since I was a little girl, I had dreamed of something romantic but tiny.

Erik, on the other hand, wanted a big wedding. And because I love Erik, I didn't want to talk him out of it. I didn't want to let him down from *his* dream.

"Let's write our guests down," I said. Just write down the most important people in our lives. So we did. And the list kept going and going. Turned out that we had a whole lot of people we loved. Erik and I both have lived in so many cities—we have friends scattered all over the country. We have large families; we have friends we still talk to from youth; huge support teams within our businesses. I'm telling you, the list just went on and on.

Erik and I looked at each other and back at this never-ending list. We were having a shared moment. You know when you look at someone and it's like you're reading each other's minds? It was clear that we were both overwhelmed by how many people we'd want to invite.

"We could just, you and me . . . get married," I said. "And let people know after it happens. I guess in a word, elope." I was kind of joking about eloping, but maybe I wasn't.

Did we really need all these people? If we wanted to get married, we should just *get married*.

There are so many expectations that families and society put on us. When you are planning a wedding, please, do not listen to every person in your life. You cannot listen to your parents. (Okay, sometimes listen to your parents. Mom's only advice on this wedding—to find a beautiful venue instead of city hall—was actually the most important twist in the entire plan. And I am so glad we listened.) You cannot listen to your friends. (Okay, take *some* advice—but for heaven's sake, don't take it all!)

Erik took another long look at the list. He heard what I was saying.

"Why were we going to wait a year to get married? So we could get everyone in a room drinking and dancing? We could do that on a Tuesday!" I said. "Let's figure out what *we* want. What if we just get married, you and me?"

Erik looked at me and gave me his dreamy little smile. "As long as our moms are there," he said, "I'm good."

Yes, that's right. That's the kind of guy I married: a guy who not only cares about his own mom but who also cares about mine.

We started dreaming up details that night, together in our room at the Bowery Hotel. First, we decided to have just our immediate families—that's about eighteen people. Then we went to the next step: location. Where did we want it?

"It has to be beautiful on its own, without my help," I said.

I spend my days making spaces beautiful and deciding every tiny detail. I didn't want to do that for our wedding day. Really, I didn't want to do much.

"I don't want to have to pick any decor. I don't want to have to worry about napkins. I don't want to talk about lighting. I just want to show up," I told him. It just had to be pretty.

Erik looked around at the beautiful hotel room we were in. "Why don't we just do it here?" he said.

And all of a sudden, it became very clear. Yes, of course. We should 100 percent do it here!

When these little lightning bolts strike, you have to jump on them. They don't come often. Your instinct will lead the way. It will allow you to create the best possible decisions for yourself, even if it seems slightly wild. And it *was* wild, what we were about to do, but it sounds wilder than it actually was. It was really just two people in love who were getting married, like millions of people in love have done before us.

Now, it was around midnight. "Call down to the front desk," I said. We needed to know if this was even possible. Did they have the space for us? Were they booked until June 2045? What the heck did it cost? We called down and left a message for the events people, giggling at our self-proclaimed genius.

———

Erik and I met in Venice, California. He walked into my backyard with a friend while a few of us were sitting around a fire. It was a beautiful California night. The truth is, there was no magic spark; there was no *uh-oh* moment. He was nothing but a nice guy in a cowboy hat, sitting across the fire in my backyard.

I do remember one thing about that night, though—I remember appreciating his energy. I remember how nice it was to hear his laughter in our backyard. I couldn't even tell you what he looked like at that moment, but he did have a glow around him. Or maybe that was just the fire pit.

After that night, my friends and I would see Erik around Venice. We'd wave to each other and be on our way.

Years later, I went to one of his Buck Mason parties. He had a tiny little store off Abbott Kinney, a shopping street in Los Angeles, that sold T-shirts and jeans, and something was different.

Erik says that he started dating me six months before I started dating him. He pursued me for a long time. We'd go out for dinner; we'd go out for drinks. We would stay out and talk all night long. No kissing;

we'd hug good night, and off he'd go. He would call me the next day to make plans for the next time we could hang out—true to his course. He was on a mission.

At first, I didn't want to kiss him. Didn't think a second thought about him; he was just a great guy that I liked to be around. In hindsight, I think I might have been fooling myself. As we talked more, as we became closer, and I started to realize what an amazing man he was, *all* I wanted was to kiss him, but I continued to wait. I knew this was different. I knew that first kiss would change the trajectory of my life. I knew if I kissed him, there was no turning back. And as I sit here writing this, with a big smile on my face and feeling our sweet little girl kicking inside of me, I'd say I was definitely right.

I say to him now, "I'm so glad you pursued me, that you knew what you wanted and that you knew better than I did."

That's just his brain. He's a conscious guy. Even three thousand miles away, I feel his presence more than I feel that of most people who are in the same room with me. He's emotionally present, and I need that. I'm an emotional human being. I feel everything. I mean, I tear up at commercials!

When we started dating, Erik said to me, "It's so wild. I feel like I've known you a million years—but also like we just met yesterday." To this day, that's how I feel about him: like we've known each other for a million years, but we just met yesterday. As Erik says every day when he gets out of bed and looks around at the amazing world that we are lucky enough to live in, *"What a life!"*

———

My little dreamy love-filled cocoon with Erik, planning our tiny romantic wedding, had one interruption. That Thursday I had to fly from

New York to Knoxville for a big shoot for HGTV. I was so busy with work that day that I couldn't even check in with Erik about updates. I just went along with my day, hoping it would work out.

That afternoon, Erik texted me the two greatest sentences: "Call me. It's all planned."

I'm sorry. *What?* The groom planned our entire wedding?

The answer: yes.

Ladies, I highly recommend you get yourself a man who can plan a wedding. Turns out that morning, while I was on the way to the airport, he walked down to the front desk and found Amanda Len, the director of special events at the Bowery Hotel, and the two of them just . . . arranged it all.

"Amanda loved our story, and she hooked us up! The wedding is Sunday evening," he said. "We can be there at 5:00 p.m. We can have the ballroom for two hours, and then we'll walk down to the restaurant, Gemma, for dinner in the private room. They're just going to give us menus and bottles of wine."

It was Thursday. Our wedding was going to be Sunday.

"Do we say go?" Erik said.

Albert Einstein is credited with saying, "You have to color outside the lines once in a while if you want to make your life a masterpiece." We're all so concerned about making everything fit in a box that someone else drew for us—especially when it comes to weddings—but life doesn't always need to work that way. Erik and I were so busy with our schedules that, for us, having a wedding in this amount of time was an amazing blessing. And let's just say we aren't scared of spontaneity. We love coloring outside the lines. In fact, let's not even color outside the lines; I say, let's make *new* lines. That's exactly what we did with this wedding.

"I love it," I said. "Let's call our moms."

Because if our moms couldn't be there, or if they weren't thrilled with this plan of ours, it was going to all lose steam real quick.

I called Mom from Knoxville. "Hi, Mom. Hiiii. Uh . . . Can you be in New York on Sunday?" I asked her.

Reminder: it was now Thursday.

"Hi, honey! . . . Huh?"

"Well, Erik and I want to get married in New York on Sunday. We just want to make sure you can be there."

Mom paused. She's known me for thirty-seven years. She knows how I operate—sometimes on the spur of the moment. But she was still trying to talk it through with me. Was I sure I wanted to have this kind of wedding? Was I sure I wanted it *right now*?

Yes, I was absolutely sure, I told her. We just want to do it. And we want to do it here.

She wasn't saying no, so that was something. "Well. What's Erik's mom saying?"

Erik's mom asked the same question: "What's Leanne's mom saying?" I think they were both hoping the other one was going to say no. Not that they didn't want us to marry each other, but I'm sure the spontaneity of it all gave them a bit of a surprise.

Of course, then we had to contact our families. Could Erik's sisters get there? Was Steve free? Could Michelle and her husband and kids pull this off? Yes. Yes. Yes. Everyone can do it. Everyone can be there Sunday.

It just seamlessly all fell in place. It was a *go*. Or more aptly, it was *go time*.

I needed a dress, and Erik also needed something to wear. He found a tuxedo down the street at a resale shop. He surprised me. I walked down the aisle to a man in a three-piece Italian tuxedo—dreamy!

I texted my assistant in LA. "I have this big, flowy dusty rose vintage dress in my closet," I wrote. "Can you overnight it to me? And also, can you send those red suede heels?" I didn't want anyone to catch on to what we were doing, so about a minute later I texted her again: "Date night!" With some kind of heart emoji or something.

Friday I got the box—a gorgeous vintage Christian Dior silk dress and perfect Alaïa heels, all shoved into a little wrinkled ball. But that sums me up perfectly. I opened it like it was a treasure chest filled with gold. And it was a treasure chest, wasn't it? My beautiful, floor-length gown was shoved in this box; out it came. My wedding dress—check. (I actually never got around to steaming it, which you can tell in pictures. Oops!)

By Friday, I was back in NYC. I forgot to mention that Saturday was the big opening of Erik's Buck Mason store, which I was helping design and install. (I know, I know. We really are crazy.)

There were a few more wedding details we had to take care of. We needed a cake, for instance! Erik and I headed to the bakery on the corner, just down the street from his store—and of course it just happened to have a famous chocolate cake. We ordered two pretty cakes: chocolate and vanilla.

Music? Check: got it covered. We hired a four-piece jazz band from Brooklyn to sing and play for a couple of hours. It's New York City—the world is your oyster.

"We need champagne on a silver tray," Amanda Len, the event director, said. "And we will have them handed out in white gloves." I'm telling you, Amanda made sure our wedding was lovely and beautiful.

What was next? Flowers. The hotel suggested a florist in the neighborhood. I practically skipped over there in my little cloud-nine world and floated into the flower shop.

"Hi! I'm getting married in two days," I said. "We need a couple of bouquets and three flower crowns for our nieces, please. Whatever you think works. Just have them match the Bowery Hotel."

The Bowery Hotel has an earthy palette with deep green velvets and dusty pinks, red drapes and leather sofas. Rich maroon tapestries hang on the wall, and murals in the lobby look worn and aged as if they've been there a hundred years. Dark wood paneling lines the walls, and the exposed wood ceilings seem as if they're straight out of an Italian tavern.

The florist nodded and said that she would pull something together to "match the Bowery." That was the extent of my flower planning.

I can't help but smile thinking about it. My bouquet looked as if I had picked it from a fall garden: deep reds and dusty roses, like my dress. Swoon. The flower girls' crowns were made of bay laurels with dusty pink roses; they carried messy bouquets of bay laurel. Erik's niece wore a lovely black lace dress, and my two little nieces wore dusty pink chiffon skirts and maroon sweaters. And, of course, I went and found them flowered Dr. Martens boots—an ode to my everyday boot. They all looked darling.

Photographer? I called my fashion photographer friends, Lowfield, that I had hired for years back in my creative direction days.

"I need a favor," I said. "Can you be in New York on Sunday? I want you two to shoot my wedding!"

I gave them complete carte blanche. I told them, "Shoot it however you want." And I meant it. They're professional photographers. They have that magic eye. I told them very specifically, "I don't need—or want—anything except to capture this moment. Just capture the night."

We weren't exactly going to the chapel to get married, but nevertheless, we needed someone official to marry us, someone who represented the two of us and our faith. My childhood Young Life leader and pastor, Chris Buda (yep, Buda!), was a really good family friend. Chris was a huge part of my childhood, good friends with my dad and our entire family, and an important part of my faith. This was a huge decision that

Erik and I were making. We wanted it to be with someone with deep connections and roots to who we were.

Buda lives in Pittsburgh, but I called him. I believe they call this a "Hail Mary."

"Chris, can you be here Sunday?" I said. "Erik and I are getting married, and we want you to officiate."

Chris came out to New York City on such short notice just to marry us. The stars aligned for us. It really did feel that way.

By Saturday night, the night before the wedding, everybody was there. Both sides of our immediate family had just met for the first time at the Buck Mason opening earlier that day. We were in this beautiful hotel. There was a fire glowing in the lobby. Everyone was thrilled and, yes, surprised.

Erik's business partner, Sasha Koehn, and his wife, Victoria, were in town for the opening of the store, so of course they were going to come to the wedding too. As an added and very magical perk, Victoria is a calligrapher. That night, in my hotel room, I wrote out an invitation that read something like this: "The pleasure of your company is requested this evening . . ." Victoria then crafted the invitations in calligraphy on the Bowery Hotel stationery. (Work with what ya got!) It also helps that their stationery looks like a European love letter. But really, there were no rules here. We didn't have paper. We didn't have letterpress. I didn't have note cards. But, hey, we had a professional calligrapher!

Erik asked the front desk for a typewriter. They had one, which cracks me up. He sat in the lobby and typed out each guest's name on the Bowery Hotel envelopes.

That night, while everyone was sleeping, we slipped the handmade invitations under each person's hotel door. That way, they'd find them first thing in the morning. They'd actually get an invitation to the wedding. It was really the magic icing on top.

Sunday morning, I was in a dream. I was so grateful that both of our families were able to be by our side. I thought of Dad. How much he would have loved Erik. How similar they are. How proud he'd be that I was picking such a great man and creating such a beautiful life for myself.

I walked down the aisle to "Let It Breathe" by the Water Liars. It was a song that summed us up to a tee.

I had my dusty rose gown on and walked toward him as he stared warmly at me. Erik later told me, "You looked like a Greek goddess that traveled from the 1920s to marry me." It was the best day of my life.

After the short, simple ceremony, we piled down the stairs into the hotel restaurant. Our wedding dinner was one big long table in a small, cozy room. We feasted on an amazingly gorgeous dinner with the wine flowing. After dinner, we all sat in the lobby in front of the fire. Our New York friends showed up and celebrated with us. It was a beautiful and, dare I say, perfect night. We are all still basking in the glow of it.

Mom, Michelle, and I always talk about how special it all turned out. Mom said we really left no detail unchecked. Erik and I reminisce about it—how we hacked the system. This is true. I really feel if we had tried to plan our wedding for a year, it wouldn't have come off so well.

Some of my friends won't get married because they don't want to deal with the wedding, and I say, "You don't have to deal with the wedding. You just have to focus on the love."

One of my favorite photos of the night is a group photo. No one is looking at the camera. Erik and I are at the end of a long wooden table filled with our families on each side. I'm smiling at Erik. He's got a serious look, like he's about to kiss me. Two candelabras glow on the wall. Straw baskets hang from the ceiling, a massive gold-framed mirror with a smoky frame behind us. A beautiful haze warms up the room. The two of us are surrounded by the people we love most in the world.

Our family. Our life. And what a life it is!

11

Be Excellent to
Each Other

Be excellent to each other, and party on dudes.

—BILL AND TED'S EXCELLENT ADVENTURE

Leanne

Today, we're taking Mom and Michelle over to Steve's place for the big reveal. We've come a long way from where we started. This space, all 1,800 square feet, was a blank slate. Actually, pretty much worse than a blank slate. There were blown-out metal factory windows that Steve called the "open air concept." No walls, no kitchen, no plumbing— literally just a bed in the middle of a raw space with a TV set screwed into the concrete wall. Let's just say my brother doesn't need much! But

I really wanted to make him a home. He wanted a place where Mom could come and visit and she wouldn't be afraid to sit down. And I wanted to create a space for Steve that was beautiful, that he could live in.

Actually, Steve had more demands than I thought, one of which was a steam shower. Fancy.

Steve

It's not the first time Leanne's designed a space for me.

Leanne designed an apartment for me years ago. I wanted a leather couch so badly. I told her, "If I can get this couch, I'll let you design the apartment." So she made the design around the couch. It was awesome. And I can't wait for this design to be revealed. I'm lucky I have her as my designer.

And for the record, I have an eye too.

Leanne

It was a great place after we were done with it! We painted the old floors and the very high ceilings black to match the black trim on the beautiful windows. We found vintage furniture to work with his new leather chesterfield sofa, including some of Grandma and Grandpa's old lights and furniture and a couple of gray Eames shell chairs. Steve made his own massive farm table that took up half of the space—in the best possible way—and was flanked by five-dollar bucket chairs. We took off the old upper kitchen cabinets and replaced them with a couple of crates that worked as shelves. We pitched the beat-up counters and replaced them with new inexpensive butcher block.

Steve

She and Mom did a proper TV-style reveal for me, even way back then. I was so happy!

Leanne

He even did his signature happy dance, which only comes out on special occasions. (It's mainly just some bopping around with a smile on his face, with an occasional wiggling.)

I love working with my brother—most of the time. There are, of course, ups and downs.

Steve

Not too many, though. If Leanne and I have a tiff, it'll last five minutes for me and then it's done—until it comes up again. I don't dwell on anything. I feel upset for a minute, and then it fades away. *Let's move on.* No hard feelings.

Leanne

Generally (except for when I'm pretty much crying), I feel the same way. Really, I'm so proud of us, Steve and me. We made it all the way to this point. Yes, we took our own individual paths, but now we're cruising on this journey together. It's very special, and we've both sacrificed a lot to make this happen. It does seem a lot like the way we'd play as kids. (He'd build the forts; I'd decorate 'em.) But it takes a tremendous amount of work to make this mutually beneficial.

It's not always so smooth. We're fighting against a couple of things here—a high-pressure situation, budgets, timelines—but birth order too! Steve's a middle child, yes, but he's the only boy, which means he's Mom's favorite. (Amiright?) And you could say he likes to be in control of situations, which is not easy because he has *me* for his sister. Being the youngest, I'm definitely what you might call free-spirited. We've got some big personalities here.

"It's not easy working with a sibling," Michelle, our older sister, said to me one day. "There are things that you would say to a sibling that you would never say to a friend or a colleague. You know each other almost too well." She's right.

Here are some strategies that have worked for us.

1. KEEP YOUR MONEY SEPARATE

The hardest part of working together—I know I've said this before, and I'll say it again—is the budget. It's what we argue most about: money.

Family businesses, despite being the backbone of this country, are notorious for ending in knock-down, drag-out fights over money. Steve and I didn't want that. When you're involved in such a big project like this—working on a television show with your older brother—you have to really think things through early.

Steve and I don't work like your average family business. He has Steve Ford Construction. I have Leanne Ford Interiors. We are separate entities, separate businesses entirely. We keep our money separate as much as humanly possible. So, we'll go into a job, and everything is signed separately. (Have I hammered home *separate* enough for you yet?)

But when we're working on the show together and we're working on these budgets, we're intertwined. Sometimes I'll say, "Well, we need more money for lighting, because three hundred dollars for twelve lights isn't going to cut it."

During season 1, we fought twice. Both times were about where the money should be spent. Only two times is pretty good stats, if you ask me! The problem was, of course, they got it all on camera. Thankfully, they edited it well, so it didn't feel as heated as it was in person. I remember those arguments well, and Steve was driving me *crazy*. But to everyone watching on TV, it was comedy.

Steve

Look: in the end we're fine. We're always fine. We're family, and she's my little sister.

2. TRUST EACH OTHER

At the end of the day, if I do what Leanne asks, I know it's going to be beautiful. Why? Because I trust her.

I might seem grumpy when we're shooting, but that's my process. I'm worried about the budget, if everything is going to happen on time. People are calling me, asking questions nonstop. So there's a lot happening behind the scenes that you don't see. Sometimes it takes me a long time to figure out how we're going to make it as beautiful as Leanne wants it to be.

Leanne

He trusts my design work, and I completely trust his carpentry work. Trust is a huge part of any business relationship. You can't have one person who is pulling more weight than the other. It just doesn't work out that way. You start to feel resentful and angry. Steve and I have a very similar work ethic. We both go full speed ahead until the work is done the right way.

The good news is that Steve always figures it out. He really does. In fact, his *worst decision* was figuring out how to help renovate my schoolhouse. The reason Steve worked on that job—and all the other jobs following that one—was because *he* was the one who figured it out.

3. CREATE BOUNDARIES

This is probably the hardest thing to do when you're working with a sibling, but you have to be able to create boundaries. (Actually, that's true in any relationship, but that's for another time.) When you work with siblings, you know what makes them tick. They know how to push your buttons. Sometimes, you get back into those old habits of being a kid, like if you were fighting over Monopoly.

Though you might want the environment to be superpersonal and easygoing, the best possible scenario is if you handle the job site and the people around you in the most professional way you can. Yes, of course you can make jokes, but at the end of the day, it's a job, and you're putting everything you have into it. You want to be serious, even though it's your sibling that you're working with. Steve and I joke around all the time on the show—you can see us ribbing each other a lot, actually—but then we're back to getting the work done.

Steve

Physical boundaries are important too. Like, say, you have a sister—*hint, hint*—who collects a lot of stuff. *Hint, hint.* And she wants to store all of her stuff in your new shop. *Hint, hint.*

I wanted to be a nice brother, so I told Leanne that she could have a space to store her stuff in the shop for the show. My first floor is 2,500 square feet; I could spare some room for her. But you have to understand: Leanne has amassed a collection over the years. She has tables and upholstered chairs, stools and couches and silverware and glasses.

I started out giving her about 200 square feet. I figured that would be enough room. But Leanne showed up here with two semi trucks full of furniture!

"Where are you going to put all of this stuff?" I said, watching it pile up in my shop.

Now there are aisles of her things, like a storage room with shelving. It's like a store in here.

I know Leanne. I knew what was going to happen—she was going to take over my space.

So I put up a Sheetrock wall. Yes I did. Boundaries, people!

The next time she came, I said, "You can't go past this wall."

And you know what? She respected that. (But if she needed more space, I'd give it to her—for a fee.)

Leanne

4. ALLOW IDEAS TO EVOLVE

I don't have a formula for design. I treat design like art. I look at a house or a room and I think, *How can I look at this differently? What can I save that already exists here?*

A house is a canvas to me. I always look for a different perspective; I am looking at the pyramid instead of just the triangle. My process is constantly evolving, and I've allowed myself to build that process and rely on it for years and years. In fact, when you let go of your original vision and let things evolve—well, that's when the good stuff happens.

Steve is more orderly than I am, probably, and maybe less open to the process of evolving. I think that's just the nature of how his mind works. He can be creative, and I know he appreciates creativity, but he's more mechanical.

Steve

For me, order is like a reset. I like to make a huge mess and then clean up the job site before we move on. Install, clean up, reset. I think I look at design jobs the same way. I want to do the job and then end the job, but most jobs don't work out that way.

Often I'll think, *How on earth are we going to do this?* My first reaction is to really resist the process. But what I need to work on is letting the idea simmer, letting it digest. Usually I'll come back to Leanne the next day, sometimes with my own ideas, and say, "Hey, you were right."

I have to be better at opening myself up to the process more. Sometimes the process isn't so black-and-white.

Leanne

And I get it! It's hard when you have a crew trying to hang on for dear life. It's also hard when you're doing fifteen homes at the same time. That's been my struggle. I don't have a design formula so that my design team can sweep in and say, "Leanne likes these five methods." Each design is custom to the clients and to their home. I give my grand plans for design, but after we demo, it naturally evolves. I have to let myself work that way, and I need that creative process. New things come up all the time—some that are *possible* and some that are *impossible*. So my design has to evolve while the show is going and while the project is opening up. If you're working with me—heaven help you—just hold on for dear life.

I know it frustrates Steve when I change the design midway, but half is out of necessity and half is because something better came along. I'd be doing the client a disservice not to be open to the evolution of the creation of a home.

Our plumber, Mike, always says to me, "What are you turning into a sink today, Leanne?" He's the one who worked on my bathroom in the schoolhouse.

I always say to him, "Mike, aren't you mad that you made that bathroom work out?" Because eight years later, he's still working on crazy design projects with me. He rolls with the punches.

That's an important point for family members and nonfamily members: be open to someone else's process.

Our electrician, who isn't a family member, is creative as well. He understands why we're moving the light an inch to the right: because it looks better! He understands that it's an art project. And if the person I hire doesn't understand why I make the decisions I make (because it's always for the good of the project), then they probably won't last. Chances are, it means they don't want to be there anyway.

Isn't it better to allow a process to evolve, too, to really allow yourself to sit in it and mull over ideas instead of making snap decisions? Yes, of course, sometimes you need to do that, but they don't call it *the creative process* for nothing. And there's worth in that creative process—it's when the good stuff happens. Don't let anyone cut that off for you.

5. KNOW WHAT YOUR DIFFERENT SKILL SETS ARE

This should be an obvious one for us. Steve's the carpenter; I'm the designer. We defer to each other when it comes to those positions. So if I bring home a giant arch, and I want Steve to hang it in a wall to make a doorway for a client . . .

Steve

Even if the wall is eight feet tall and the arch is ten feet tall . . .

Leanne

Then I know he's going to make it work! Right, Steve? (Side note: I was right. That arch was perfect.)

Steve

Uh . . .

Leanne

See how easy that is?

Steve and I have also learned a great deal along the way about how to treat other people. Mom and Dad gave us a firm foundation in how to get around in the world, but sometimes people and situations get thrown at you where you have to think on your feet quite a bit. How we interact with other people is a big part of how we evolve into unique beings.

Last week, I was at a meet and greet for PPG paints at a store near my home. I went to this store not thinking many people would show up, but thank goodness, people were there. People of all ages, standing in line to see *me*! The show has given us so many new opportunities to meet people who really have responded to our style and our show. It's so incredible to meet people who love our work and are inspired by it. It's amazing how many people—complete strangers—want to connect with us. We do have design in common, so that helps.

I try to make sure that I make eye contact with every single person I speak with. I really do. Eye contact is a very powerful tool that humans have and that we often either don't notice or don't take advantage of.

I remember doing this as a camp counselor as well. Part of my job was reaching out to the campers and making sure they felt comfortable. I'd walk through camp and make sure to say hello to everyone I passed by: "Hi! How's your day going?" It became something of a habit, reaching out and looking someone in the eye.

When I moved to New York City, I kept it up. I know that people think of New York City as a place where people are just whizzing by each other, but believe me: when you're on city streets—whether there's only one other person on the street or you're in a crowded area—you want to have that connection. You want to know who's around you—for safety reasons, yes, but also for connection. Eye contact is a small reminder that we are not alone in all of this.

If I was walking down a city street and made eye contact with someone, I would always smile. Sometimes I would even wave. Maybe even say, "How's it going?" People are so shocked by it, but if you think about it, our instinct is to interact, not avoid. It's nice to have human connection in the tiniest way.

My friends would all make fun of me: "You aren't at summer camp anymore, girl." But I thought, *Who cares? This might be the only interaction these people feel today.*

So I started doing this with everybody. I purposely looked for eye contact. Then, if I locked eyes with someone, I'd smile. And then they'd smile.

Steve

The show hasn't gotten that big (yet?), but knowing that it might does scare me. Losing my anonymity—especially around here, because I'm such a hometown boy—is going to be hard for me. Also, I don't exactly sink into the background. I'm a giant. I'm a foot taller in a crowd!

Just the other day at a coffee shop in Pittsburgh, a woman sitting next to me spoke to me. "Are you that guy from the HGTV decorating show?" Yes, that's me.

I'm typically a pretty introverted guy, and usually people want to talk to Leanne. I keep it short because I can be shy. But I looked her in the eye, and you know what? We had a pretty good conversation.

Leanne

When I first signed up for the show, my biggest fear was losing my privacy. I was nervous to lose that right. My saving grace, mentally, is that thousands of people are on TV. We are only on television for literally a few hours, in the grand scheme of things. That's it. And there are something like six hundred channels out there. There's a ton of us—a lot of shows. Most people don't recognize us outside of Pittsburgh. Here, we're on our home turf, and Pittsburgh loves its own. But in LA and in New York, we're just faces in the crowd.

I had this image of people stopping me in the airport. In the airport, I'm dirty, I'm tired, I'm hurrying—let's just say I'm not at the top of my game. But for some reason, getting recognized at the airport happens a lot. Now, I just make sure I shower before I go. Novel idea, I know.

One time I was sitting on an airplane and had my sweatshirt on backward, so I could use my hood as a sort of sleeping mask. I had a big old spread of airplane food, and I was crying at whatever Nicholas Sparks movie was on my computer.

And the guy sitting next to me said, with a big smile on his face, "Are you Leanne Ford?" Eeek!

I spoke to a good friend about this recently. That I was worried about this privacy issue more now, knowing that season 2 was coming out. I didn't want being recognized to somehow ruin how I feel about making eye contact with people. I was concerned that this kind of attention would be, in a way, overwhelming or intrusive.

"Actually, Leanne," she said, "think about how much you love to make people feel good. This is an opportunity to connect with people. You used to say hi to people or smile at strangers all the time. Now you have this opportunity to do that more often with *more* people. You have a chance to make their day."

I liked that concept. I heard that. I always think about that perspective now when someone approaches me. That's a pretty darn fun ability to have! I know it feels good because I still get giggly when I think about my favorite personalities that I've met.

When I was in my early twenties, my friend looked at me and said, "You are *so* Annie Hall." I had never heard of the movie *Annie Hall*, so I didn't know what that meant. I rented it and realized as I was watching it, *Oh my gosh, I* am *Annie Hall*. She dressed like a boy (her choice, by the way, not the choice of the costume designer for the movie). She said "La-di-da." Her face, the way she spoke, her voice, those hats—we were two peas in a pod, if I do say so myself. *That woman*, I thought, *is my celebrity soul sister.*

There really is no other celebrity that I relate to. I don't look like any of them. I don't act like any of them. I don't dress like any of them. And all of a sudden, there was somebody in a movie—Diane Keaton—that I related to. Of course, it was from 1977, but what did I care? I thought, *My goodness, we do kind of look alike. There are similarities.*

Then people would start saying to me, "You look like Diane Keaton." I just thought it was the best compliment ever. She's got her own unique look, and I was totally fine with that. I never related to the girl with a bunch of makeup on. I love that my celebrity look-alike is around thirty years older than me!

Recently, I received an email that read: "You're invited to a party for Diane Keaton's new book, *The House That Pinterest Built.*"

Diane. Keaton.

I was thrilled. I sent the email to my sister and Erik, with the subject line "AHHHHHHHHHHH."

What do I wear to meet Diane Keaton? Which hat? Which boots?

I dressed in my vintage-style suede high boots and my black limo driver hat, of course. It was a little Diane Keaton–esque.

I was legitimately nervous. Erik came with me to the party, and as soon as we walked in the door, the hostess throwing the party grabbed my hand and told me she was going to introduce me to Diane. They beelined us right over to her.

Again: Diane. Keaton.

"Hi, Diane! I'm Leanne. I'm so happy to meet you," I said.

"Oh, *you're* cute!" she said to me in her Diane Keaton way.

"Funny you should say that . . . because everybody seems to think I look like you."

She loved that! She laughed and smiled, and then she turned to Erik.

"Oh, and you're cute too!" she said to him. And then I swear to you, Diane Keaton started flirting with Erik. I was dying. It was *too good.*

"Okay, *okay. Cool* it, you two," I said. "Break it up. Break it up."

Someone started taking pictures of us. I turned to Diane, looked her in the eye. "Let's look like we're old friends," I said.

"Perfect," she said. "Let's just giggle."

Then Diane Keaton got pulled away. I was as happy as a clam. It's now a year later, and I'm still on cloud nine from the experience. A *four-minute* experience! But meeting her in person had made an impression. It made my day.

If being on this television show has taught me anything, it's that people are looking for connection to each other.

Look 'em in the eye!

WORKING ON PROGRESS

What if you used eye contact in your everyday life? What if you made eye contact with strangers—just because?

Instead of walking into the grocery store and zipping out—what if you looked up at someone in the aisle? What if you asked the clerk how her day is going? What if the two of you made a simple human connection that might really affect her, and you in return? What if that simple eye contact led to a smile? It would give you a positive pause from all the chaos in everyday life, and it takes only three seconds.

12

Ignore Everyone

Don't think about making art, just get it
done. Let everyone else decide if it's good or
bad, whether they love it or hate it. While
they're deciding, make even more art.

—ANDY WARHOL

Leanne

There's something Steve and I have both noticed we do that seems to
be working quite well for us: we tend to ignore everyone.

It sounds more aggressive than it really is. It's a simple concept.
You know what you need, what you like, what you love, what you
think looks good, what you think feels right, and what you believe in
more than anyone else does. The second we start listening to outside

opinions chiming in on what we should and shouldn't do—that's when we get cloudy.

Now, this is not to say don't take counsel from those you trust, because, yes, that can be important and effective to your growth. But the key word there is *trust*.

Don't listen to naysayers. Don't listen to strangers who comment on your Instagram, saying they would *never* use that paint color. Ignore the low-self-esteem kids trying to bring you down to their level. Ignore the voice inside you telling you that you really must get married before a certain age. Ignore the magazine telling you your kitchen tile and your favorite dress are now "out."

Wear it anyway; paint it anyway; love it anyway; do it anyway.

It's "You Do You" on a large scale—and it changes everything.

You have to know when and what to ignore. That goes for the comments on the internet too. People ask us about that a lot now that we're in the public eye.

At the beginning of our journey, when the show first aired, Michelle warned Mom, "Don't read the comments on anything about Leanne and Steve because you're going to get upset, and some of them are just plain mean."

Others warned her too. Not everyone was going to be in love with the work we did, and they were going to let it be known.

People ask me a lot if I look at the comments that people have about my design. I'm going to be honest with you: I don't even know most of the comments exist. I've never tried to read all of them or take them too seriously, whether they're good or bad.

It can be tricky. I like to connect with people, so I am on my personal page. If I have talked to you on there, yes, that's really me. But I generally find that my Instagram has a lot of love to it. Design Instagram is pretty tame. If you're all revved up about the color I chose for a sofa, life's okay.

There was one lady who said something mean about an artist whose work I posted. "Oh, you deleted my comment?" she wrote.

I replied, "Yes, because this is my account, which means this is *my* house. And insulting an artist and his or her work is just so unnecessary."

People aren't going to like everything you do. Art is subjective. You don't have to like what I create. But why comment on what you don't like? What purpose does that serve? There are a million designs that I feel no affinity toward. I don't have to comment on them. They don't need to know that. It's just not meant for me. It's meant for a different audience.

Steve

The thing I don't like about social media is that it's everybody's highlight reel. I can be having a great day. Maybe I sit down and hop on Instagram and start scrolling. All of a sudden, I realize that everyone is on vacation. Like, that's all anyone is doing in the world. Everyone's on vacation or having fun, except for me. Then it makes you feel bad that your life isn't as interesting.

I have to take a step back and say, "Hey, wait a minute. My life is awesome too. Isn't it?"

Leanne

Who cares what the cranky guy sitting on his laptop in his basement has to say about my designs, when I'm out there in the world actually trying to make something? I'm living my life. The reason people don't do or make anything is because they are nervous of what people are going to think. That's such a waste. One bad thing cannot take away from the ten good comments; it can't take away from the people whose lives we made happier.

Do I look like the happiest person on social media? Yes, I'm sure I do. But you edit your life the way you want to on social media. I make it look good. I used to be a stylist, and now I'm a decorator—that's my *job* to make it look good.

The key is, we all have to remember that when we're scrolling on social media, this is an edited version of life. You have to give yourself a break.

Social media is deeply rooted in our lives. I wish I could say, "Don't look," but it's part of how we now communicate as a culture. It's how I communicate with other artists. It's how I communicate in my business. The bottom line is, are someone else's opinions going to make me, or you, or any of us, stop creating? Stop being on TV? Stop making art?

Absolutely not.

When you put yourself out there as an artist, you always leave yourself susceptible to criticism. You do have to develop a thicker skin. That isn't always easy, and it can take years to do.

For me, creating is breathing. I can't live without creating; this is what I do. Whether people like it or not, this is who I am.

———

I've spoken to my fair share of people over the past few years: interviews, design discussions, promoting a product I've gotten behind because I've fallen in love with it. And people ask me all the time, "What are the new trends?"

I don't answer that question, except to say, "Ignore them all."

I know this might sound very against the decorating grain. That there are trends in the design world, and we are supposed to embrace them. Wrong.

For one, I could name five different trends, and by the time you read this book and then decide to go out and buy an item based on the trend that I told you was hot, that trend will most likely be over. Trends constantly come and go.

Remember Mom's living room, which I detailed earlier? She kept an Asian theme in her living room for twenty years. She's been in and out of the "right" trend (whatever that means) so many times I can't even count.

What about the refrigerator that I painted white? That refrigerator was avocado! Someone decided to sell those refrigerators because that was a hot color at the end of the 1970s, and people bought them.

Just because someone deemed it to be popular, and just because it's in every book or blog or magazine, does not mean that you are going to connect with it. It doesn't mean that you are going to want that trend in your home.

When I decorate, I use a blend of styles. I mix Italian high-end chairs with handmade crafts and beat-up tables all the time. I use poured concrete with white-washed brick. I strip down wood so it looks raw, and I paint exposed beams so they look about a hundred years old. I made my coffee table in my home from a mirrored platform from an old discotheque. I really believe this mix of items—I'll call it my *un-trend* quality, if you will—makes my designs approachable. My aesthetic doesn't follow a rule.

A lot of trends start with people just breaking rules—or better yet, making up the rules themselves. My theory on trends is simple: people get bored. We all get bored of that same kitchen or those same sandals. The "tastemakers" are really just the first ones to get bored.

It's true! They get bored and go on the hunt for something new to inspire them.

Isn't that how Birkenstocks came back into fashion? When I was wearing Birkenstocks, my sister thought I was crazy. She laughed at me!

"In two years, you're going to be wearing these Birkenstocks," I said. Sure enough, she's wearing them, because they became a trend. And her kids are wearing them too!

I'm not saying that I created the Birkenstock trend—though I might have helped get the trend going in my little hometown—but something about Birkenstocks reinvaded the culture.

This happens in the design world all the time—the tide shifts. And it takes time for people to get used to a new design. They need to see the design or the fashion, or even a different way of thinking, enough times to let it sink in. Do you think the trend of having an open floor plan in a house just came about overnight? Of course not. The open floor plan evolved out of necessity because families changed. Suddenly there was just no need for a formal living room, so homes evolved. Walls started coming down. People were more interested in roomy, cozy kitchens. This never would have happened twenty-five years ago—and even as I write this, designers and clients are leaning back toward smaller rooms and closed doors.

This brings me to Michelle's red brick fireplace in her kitchen. It was very dark, and I wanted her to paint it. I *insisted* she paint it. But she was terrified.

"How can you paint brick?" she would say.

Easy—with a can of white paint!

She had seen all the white paint I used so successfully. She had seen my house. She had seen the other houses that I had painted white. She loved them all, but this was different. She was afraid that the brick shouldn't be painted over.

There are camps around painting brick. Some people can't even imagine doing it. Others embrace it. My sister was not embracing it.

"Leanne, I don't know how I feel about painting brick," she kept saying. "You can't reverse that."

(Side note: Yes, you—kind of—can.)

Michelle talked to Mom about it. "Leanne said it would be beautiful," Mom told her. "So it'll be beautiful."

But my sister talked about it and talked about it and talked about it . . . for five long years. She agonized over it.

I'm here to tell you that if you own your house, you can do whatever the heck you want. You have to think of the greater cause of the room. In my sister's case, she had to think about the greater cause of her kitchen, which meant that brick fireplace was going to look better white.

Five years later—five years!—she finally agreed to it. And you know what? She loved it. The room looked prettier and bigger.

"Why didn't we do this earlier?" she said.

Michelle!

You are your own person. You're not defined by a trend, and trends don't define you. I say ignore the trends and create your *own* look. Play a little, as Steve and I like to say. Get wild. Who knows? Maybe you'll be the one to start a new trend.

———

We all get distracted by the voices all around us and the voices in our heads. *You're not good enough. You're not cool enough. You're not interesting.* The way social media encourages us to look around ourselves all the time instead of inside ourselves can inflate those feelings. Do yourself a favor: ignore most people—even me!—and only pay attention to the very few people in your life whose opinions really matter. We're not here on this earth to sit around and spend our time worrying about who we are in other people's eyes. We're here to spread love and kindness and create a world for others and for ourselves that feels good, not to compare ourselves to others and not to allow another person's negative words to take us down.

13

Leanneisms

The difference between weird and wonderful is just good design.

—LEANNE FORD

Leanne

I know there are a lot of creative souls out there reading this who are just starting out on their creative lives. Maybe you are still in high school and have to just get through math class. (Who needs it, really? Hi, calculators!) Or maybe you are a mother or father of three kids, doing a job you don't love in a career you don't care about. It is never too early or too late to follow your dream or even to think of a new dream.

I'm a designer. It would be crazy for me not to have a chapter on design. I want to tell you that I have *all* the answers to your design problems, that if you do this one little thing, your house is going to look like one in a magazine. But you know I don't believe in any formula like that.

You know what I believe in? I believe you—and everyone—should love their homes.

That's it. Yes, really. That is it. You and your family, the ones living in your home, are the only ones who matter.

I look at a house as a blueprint without interior walls. I get tunnel vision and focus on what needs to move. Move your bathroom to the back of your house? Yes! Move the living room to the front of your house? Yes! Take out the staircase and put in an entirely new staircase? Yes!

People who are trying to convince you *out* of your dream will say that they are doing so because they want *you* to be happy. That taking a risk is hard, too hard.

I say no. How will you ever know what is going to look good in your home if you don't follow your own path?

Here are a couple of ideas to make your house your favorite design project—and your dream home.

1. ADD ART TO YOUR HOME

I'm a huge fan of installing art in my homes and the homes I decorate. In my new 1950s personal project, I commissioned my friend Elaina Sullivan to create an enormous white painting that is hanging on my white wall for the entryway of my house.

Remember: you can frame anything and say it's art. I will frame doodles from friends, magazine tear sheets, or ripped-out pictures from books I love. Anything that makes my little heart happy.

Probably the biggest risk I took with an art installation was for the Yanakos family. Pittsburgh artist Carolyn Kelly custom painted their entryway stairs in a high-gloss black and then painted a white high-gloss graffiti-like design over the steps. The client requested those stairs specifically; they were inspired by a previous project I had done with the same artist.

"You can name my firstborn child if I get to have graffiti stairs," the owner said to me.

Okay, great. Let's do graffiti stairs. And her name shall be Bongo.

I posted the finished product on my Instagram, and my goodness, those stairs were so polarizing. Some people loved it; some hated it. But the only opinion that mattered was my clients', because it was their house and they had to live in it. They were thrilled.

I'll say it again: art is subjective. That's why I love it. I've always been in an industry where someone is almost always going to like my work and someone is not. And if no one hates it, then it's most likely that no one loves it.

You and your family live in the house, and your family is going to live with the art. If you decide that you want to draw on your wall—go for it. You can always paint over it. But don't stop yourself from taking that risk because you're worried about what other people are going to think.

2. CREATE A SOLUTION OUT OF A PROBLEM

The farmhouse I lived in for a short time was a wreck when I first got it. I ripped down walls, painted everything white—you know the drill—and that's not so hard to do. But I had an attic that I loved and wanted to use as a room. That was the good thing. The problem was getting to it.

In the second-floor hallway, there were two closets and the attic pull-down staircase. I don't like wasting space in a house; if the space is there, I want to use it. I wanted the attic to be a full office. Here was the big problem: How would I turn this into an everyday room?

So I spoke to Ed Zeiler and Steve. Ed has been friends with Steve for more than ten years, and he's an incredible woodworker. I told him what my idea was: to have a wooden spiral staircase. It couldn't take up any room, so we had to get creative. I wanted something artistic and beautiful. Ed, who's a regular on the show now, majored in photography in college and minored in sculpture. His dad had a remodeling company when he was growing up as well. We've all been really lucky to have Ed in our lives and to take risks on projects with us. He's a true talent.

"That staircase was one of the hardest things I've ever built," Ed said. He built the whole staircase in his shop—all hand-carved, hand-bent wood; each stair had a different cut. I loved that staircase—it was like a piece of artwork. We ripped out the closets, closed up the pull-down attic, and installed that staircase. It was a huge job.

I say this all the time, but some of the most beautiful design elements in my homes, or in the homes I work on, were created as a solution to a problem. That staircase is no exception.

3. *THEIR* HEIRLOOMS DON'T HAVE TO BE *YOUR* HEIRLOOMS

Imagine this scenario: Grandma gave Mom a giant velvet-painted portrait. "This is a collectible. You have to keep it," she says. But Mom doesn't like it, and it doesn't fit in her house. She doesn't know what to do with it. She feels guilty about getting rid of it. She gives it to you. Now you're stuck with the burden of carrying this giant velvet-painted portrait for fifty years. And guess what? You're going to pass it on to your kid, who's still not going to want it. And the cycle continues, a long line of torturing the next family member.

Here's an idea: just get rid of it. You don't *have* to keep the family heirloom.

What looked great in Grandma's house isn't always going to look great in your house, and that's okay. If you love it, great! If it's not your style, don't keep it. I see it over and over again on the show and in people's homes: because they're still holding on to these heirlooms, they never fully move in and make a place their own. Which means they never get to love where they live. It's this vicious cycle we all trick each other into.

You have full permission to purge what you don't want.

Your home should have your energy and your soul. It has to have your intention, your purpose. Make conscious choices for your home. Only bring in what brings you and your family joy.

4. ALWAYS ADD VINTAGE

I have a friend who hired an interior designer. I walked into her home, excited to see the transformation, but once I walked in that door, my excitement just dropped. It wasn't the design; it was nice enough, and everyone has different tastes. I don't judge if you want to do your entire home in any style as long as that's what *you* want. But a good interior designer should lead you in a direction where the home represents who you are.

We have lots of layers within us. We have history. We've been on trips. We have old and new.

When I walked into my friend's house, I looked around in shock because everything was brand-new and store bought. Every single piece of art, every piece of furniture, every rug—all new and easy to find. It was almost like the designer was just trying to check the design project off their list. It was missing the soul, the fire, the oomph. It needed some heart.

That's where vintage comes in. I believe deeply in mixing in vintage. You don't have to do *all* vintage, but it's good to represent the stories of life through your decorating choices. If someone is picking out all new furniture, all new items, all new knickknacks for your house, it becomes a house without a soul.

That's how my friend's house felt. It didn't represent her and who she was as a person. Her tastes, her dreams. The decor could have been anywhere. It could have belonged to anyone. It was the first time I saw a home so obviously missing that element.

Don't worry—we did some quick work and fixed her place up, adding soul with some vintage pieces and mixing it in with the new. Now she loves her home.

5. WEAR BLACK, PAINT WHITE

You knew this one was coming, didn't you?

Don't underestimate the power of white paint. It is the most universal, most forgiving, most timeless, classic, and beautiful color you can use in your home. It is failproof, and it works in your home. I promise.

In fact, I really love paint as a general tool in home design. Anything can be painted. I have painted new furniture, painted mirrors, painted sofas, painted floors—you name it. (I've even painted Tom Ford the dog. Not on purpose—I mean, I asked him to move!) But don't forget about this option to freshen up your home. It's easy and budget friendly and can make a huge difference. It's amazing how a good coat of fresh paint can spruce things up.

6. DESIGN LIKE A CREATIVE DIRECTOR

Always think of the best visual in a room. What's the best thing going about that space? Is it the windows? The fireplace? The bathtub? Design the room around that focal point. Think of "the shot" when working on your space, because that's what you will see every day.

I'm working on a house right now that you'll see in season 2 of the show. The master bathroom was a mess. First of all, the toilet was the first thing you saw when you walked into the bathroom. This was a problem! My client also had a beautiful copper tub that she didn't know what to do with. I knew exactly what to do with it: make it the focus of the room. I always take the prettiest item and make that the centerpiece of the room.

So we moved the tub, and then we moved the toilet behind the door. Now, when you walk into the master bathroom, you see their magnificent copper tub, and it changes everything.

7. TAKE SOME PICTURES

If you want to get into design, then by all means, start taking pictures of your work! I know making a look book isn't actually a design tip, but if you're going to work so hard on making your home beautiful, it's important to take photos. You want to document your progress.

I realized that anyone who was going to hire me was going to ask me if I had a book to look at. If you want to get into interior design—which people ask me about all the time—you absolutely have to start by making a book. People want to see what you can do and why they should hire you. They need visual proof. I can't stress this enough.

You've only decorated your own house? That's fine! Rearrange your bedroom and take pictures. Or rearrange the plates and the trinkets in your kitchen. Rearrange your friend's bedroom. Take lots of pictures, and take risks with your ideas. Your style and your aesthetic will always evolve, and it will always get better. Take some pictures one way; then move a chair or place a new blanket down. Do an edit—that's exactly what magazines do.

Study your favorite interior magazines and books and dissect what you love about the pictures. Is the chair pulled out from under the table?

Is the floral arrangement off-center? Then re-create your favorite tricks in your own pictures.

My career in design started taking off when people started asking me to do little projects for them. I never said no (say *yes* until you get to say *no*), and I took pictures of everything. If I got *one* great picture out of the project, it was worth it. I went in with my creative director marketing brain, thinking of the imagery.

Think about the end visual. What do you want it to look like? What's the best angle? Highlight the prettiest, most interesting pieces, in the best angles. Cheat the furniture. (Move it forward; move it back. A chair can sit in the middle of the room for a picture, even if you don't live with it in that position.) Do what you need to do to get the shot. You're creating art; do what you have to in order to make it special. Put your camera on a tripod or a table, and let the natural light in.

Maybe a hundred people ever get to be in that house, but thousands can potentially see a picture of it. The more people that can enjoy your work, the better.

14

So Far. So Good.

There is a vitality, a life force, an energy, a quickening that
is translated through you into action, and because there
is only one of you in all of time, this expression is unique.
And if you block it, it will never exist through any other
medium and it will be lost. The world will not have it.

−MARTHA GRAHAM

Leanne

I hear them constantly, the what-ifs: "But what if it doesn't work? What
if we don't like the color? What if I buy a rug too small? What if I buy
furniture that's too big? What if . . ."

Why are we so afraid to fail? Who taught us that fear? We aren't
born with fear. Have you ever seen kids' artwork? It's amazing—free

of all inhibitions and worry. Why do we stop painting like that? When do we stop trying out new ideas? Or a new rug, for that matter? When do we start worrying?

And what is failure anyway? What if failure is just a loving and kind nudge for us toward where we were supposed to be in the first place? What if it's just a plot twist?

A failed career path? Great. Seems like you really weren't supposed to be doing that job in the first place, or at least you aren't supposed to do it anymore.

A failed relationship? Maybe what you gained from it and how you grew from it are so powerful that, though it ended, it's actually just a twisted version of your biggest success story.

A failed art piece? Someone might think it's the most beautiful thing they've ever seen.

I have grown to love failure. Once you see through the weeds and let your ego take a hike, you realize this is all for your own good, your own progress, and it's all pushing you to where you are supposed to be, to whom you are supposed to be with, and even to who you are supposed to be.

So many of us are frightened and, dare I say, paralyzed by the fear of messing up. It stops us from trying something new, creating something we have never seen, pushing ourselves to break limits in any way. That fear is blowing it. It's stopping us from seeing what we can become, what we can create, how much we can accomplish in our short little time here on the planet.

It doesn't matter if the thing I tried worked. In fact, personally I almost love when it *doesn't* work sometimes. It allows me to check it off my list. *Welp, I am not supposed to be a photographer; that's for sure. Nope, this city is not for me; that's one less city I have to daydream about.*

What if we flip the script? What if we fail up and fail often, fail *on purpose*, just to see that it doesn't really hurt as badly as we imagined it would? And what if we support each other through the failure, encouraging others to try new things and giving them a high five when it doesn't work as planned? Because just trying something new and different in any way deserves a high five.

Did you know Dr. Seuss's first book for kids was rejected twenty-seven times?[1] He seems to have turned out fine.

Steve

I'm a big believer that if you mess up, just keep trying to figure it out, no matter how much time it takes. I think people give up too easily.

In my world, I'm working with all sorts of crews, and we're coming together to create something that's special and custom for our clients. That's not easy, and humans aren't perfect. We do our best, but sometimes it's try, try, try—and one more try—again. You have to give yourself the chance to learn from your mistakes, and that's okay. In my case, mistakes can be expensive and a waste of time, and yes, that's a total drag; believe me. But it's part of the process.

One of the most important factors in my success has been having some outstanding mentors who have helped me along the way. While I'm still being mentored, I'm always learning something new. Now I'm enjoying being a mentor myself. Dang—how did that happen?

I appreciate those people who took time to invest in me as I was learning my craft. I learned so much about carpentry and construction from some great guys who took me under their wings when I first started. I'm thankful for that. And now I feel like it's my opportunity to do the same for others. I want to keep training people and helping them become better. That's what makes my job interesting.

I love that about the show and my work on *Restored by the Fords*. With so many demands, we're in the trenches together, including the amazing production crew. So much time, effort, skill, and perseverance are required to create each one of those episodes. It really goes to show you that you need to be in a mind-set that is open to constantly learning and sharing.

Don't hold yourself back. Just admit it: you're going to blow it, and that's okay. When you go for it, give it all you've got, and ask for help along the way.

I also want to make sure it's really clear how hard we both have worked along the way. Leanne and I have been so lucky to have parents who were able to help us financially, yes. We've had privileges that other people aren't given. But I've also lived off my credit card before. I've scratched my way through a lot of jobs to buy my first car or to make payment for rent.

I really give my dad credit for the work ethic I have today. He always pushed us to try and to keep trying. He gave me all of the skill sets that I needed before he died, and that included never giving up, even if you feel like you're at your lowest point.

Leanne

You'll never do greatly if you don't try greatly, and that means being willing to fail greatly. Failure is the best sign that you are trying. Without all of the people throughout history who were willing to fail, we would still be sitting around a fire in a cave somewhere.

In fact, failure is nothing but change. It's nothing but an evolution. When something doesn't work, you are forced to evolve (grow!) into something else, something inevitably better. I say fail hard and fail often.

Who has encouraged you along the way? Who popped into your head while reading this book? People who have pushed you forward into the path you are in? Thank them!

Who could stand some encouragement—someone you know who has "it" but needs to hear that from someone else? Call them; tell them; hire them; help them push forward with what they are supposed to create, how they are supposed to live.

What is it you are supposed to be doing in your life? Are you doing it? Be honest with yourself. I know the answer just popped into your head; listen to it. Don't ignore your call. What can you do to push forward to getting there, wherever *there* may be? If you are like me, this may change over time; in fact, it may have already changed. And that's okay. Keep going. Keep evolving. Don't fight it. Enjoy it; be excited by it.

Go. Don't stay stagnant. Whatever your goal in life is—whether it's love, career, family, helping others, creating—go toward it now.

I had a needlepoint hanging in my room as a kid. It read, "Be Patient. God isn't finished with me yet." We are all wonderful works in progress.

So far. So good.

Notes

PROLOGUE: NEVER TOO LATE

1. Bill Daley, "A Towering Legacy," *Chicago Tribune*, August 15, 2012, https://www.chicagotribune.com/living/ct-xpm-2012–08–15-sc-food -0810-giant-child-20120815-story.html.
2. Todd Van Luling, "8 Things You Didn't Know About the Artist Vincent Van Gogh," *HuffPost*, updated December 6, 2017, https://www .huffingtonpost.com/2015/07/29/vincent-van-gogh-trivia_n_6181630 .html.
3. See Benjamin Voigt, "Robert Frost 101," Poetry Foundation, January 19, 2016, https://www.poetryfoundation.org/articles/70308/robert-frost -101; "Robert Frost Dies at 88; Kennedy Leads in Tribute," special to the *New York Times*, On This Day, January 30, 1963, https://archive.nytimes .com/www.nytimes.com/learning/general/onthisday/bday/0326.html.

CHAPTER 1: AVOCADO BE GONE!

1. See Fred Rogers, *You Are Special: Words of Wisdom for All Ages from a Beloved Neighbor* (New York: Penguin, 1995).

CHAPTER 2: GROW SLOW

1. Austin Carr, "The Most Important Leadership Quality for CEOs? Creativity," *Fast Company*, May 18, 2010, https://www.fastcompany.com /1648943/most-important-leadership-quality-ceos-creativity.

2. Adam Grant, *Originals: How Non-Conformists Move the World* (New York: Penguin, 2016), 253.
3. Grant, 164.
4. "Help & Support: Understanding the Bullying Cycle," BulliesOut, accessed February 22, 2019, https://bulliesout.com/need-support/young -people/helping-someone-else/understanding-the-bullying-cycle/.
5. CDC National Center for HIV/AIDS, Viral Hepatitis, STD, and TB Prevention and Division of Adolescent and School Health, *Youth Risk Behavior Survey: Data Summary & Trends Report 2007–2017*, 31, https ://www.cdc.gov/healthyyouth/data/yrbs/pdf/trendsreport.pdf. For more information on bullying, see https://www.stopbullying.gov/.

CHAPTER 4: SHOW UP ANYWAY

1. William Shakespeare, *Twelfth Night*, act 1, sc. 1.
2. Layla Ilchi, "10 Unforgettable Marc Jacobs Runway Moments," WWD, February 12, 2019, https://wwd.com/fashion-news/fashion-scoops /marc-jacobs-runway-fashion-week-moments-1202994209/.
3. Alana Horowitz, "15 People Who Were Fired Before They Became Filthy Rich," *Business Insider*, April 25, 2011, https://www .businessinsider.com/15-people-who-were-fired-before-they-became -filthy-rich-2011-4.
4. Lilith Hardie Lupica, "Anna Wintour Was Once Fired from Her Styling Job, Says It Was Character Building," *Vogue*, October 31, 2017, https://www.vogue.com.au/vogue-codes/news/anna-wintour-was -once-fired-from-her-styling-job-says-it-was-character-building /news-story/5309765e5cb67b6acd026f2d88c18026.

CHAPTER 7: NO GUTS, NO STORY

1. Léonie Shinn-Morris, "10 Things You Might Not Know About Vincent van Gogh," Google Arts & Culture, accessed February 25, 2019.
2. Adam Grant, "The Surprising Habits of Original Thinkers," 2016, TED video, 11:53.
3. Russell Herman Conwell and Robert Shackleton, *Acres of Diamonds* (New York: Harper & Brothers, 1915), 4–8.

CHAPTER 14: SO FAR. SO GOOD.

1. NPR staff, "How Dr. Seuss Got His Start 'On Mulberry Street,'" NPR, January 24, 2012, https://www.npr.org/2012/01/24/145471724/how-dr-seuss-got-his-start-on-mulberry-street.

About the Authors

LEANNE FORD is an American interior designer from Pittsburgh, Pennsylvania. Her easy vibe and personal style match the stylish yet approachable spaces she creates and curates. Her work has been featured in *Architectural Digest, Country Living, Domino, GQ, Lonny, Elle Decor, Martha Stewart, Better Homes and Gardens, Redbook, MyDomaine, Refinery 29*, and the *New York Times*. She is currently the star, along with her brother and contractor Steve Ford, of *Restored by the Fords* on HGTV, which follows the siblings as they turn some of Pittsburgh's most dated buildings into magazine-worthy homes.

STEVE FORD stars alongside his younger sister, Leanne Ford, on HGTV's *Restored by the Fords*. A licensed contractor and man-of-many-talents, Steve takes on the most unconventional construction challenges to bring his sister's unique interior decorating vision to life. His portfolio includes store design, displays and set design for a number of national retail brands, as well as restoration of corporate headquarters, restaurant design, and residential renovations. Steve's construction work has been featured in a variety of national decorating and home interior magazines, including *This Old House, Domino*, and *Country Living*.